Library of
Davidson College

DEGENERATION AND REGENERATION

TEXTS OF THE PREMODERN ERA

A TWENTY-NINE-VOLUME FACSIMILE SERIES
REPRESENTING THE HIGHLY VARIED
CULTURAL THEMES OF THE 1890S IN
PROSE AND POETRY

EDITED BY
**IAN FLETCHER &
JOHN STOKES**

GARLAND PUBLISHING

PLAYHOUSE IMPRESSIONS

A. B. Walkley

Garland Publishing, Inc., New York & London

1984

This facsimile has been made
from a copy in the
Yale University Library.

809.2
W186p

Library of Congress Cataloging in Publication Data

Walkley, Arthur Bingham, 1855–1926.
Playhouse impressions.

(Degeneration and regeneration)
Reprint. Originally published: London :
T. F. Unwin, 1892.
1. Drama—History and criticism—Addresses, essays,
lectures.   2. Theater—Great Britain—Addresses, essays,
lectures.   I. Title.   II. Series.
PN1623.W3   1984   809.2   82-49102
ISBN 0-8240-5565-9 (alk. paper)

84-7021
The volumes in this series are printed on
acid-free, 250-year-life paper.

Printed in the United States of America

PLAYHOUSE IMPRESSIONS

PLAYHOUSE IMPRESSIONS

BY
A. B. WALKLEY

𝔏𝔬𝔫𝔡𝔬𝔫
T. FISHER UNWIN
PATERNOSTER SQUARE
MDCCOXCII

PREFATORY NOTE.

THIS is a book of reprints. About half the articles are from the Speaker; *the rest (except one from* Black and White, *and a fragment from the* Illustrated London News) *are from the* National Observer *and the* Star. *To the several editors who have courteously sanctioned their republication I tender grateful thanks.*

As essays in dramatic criticism they do not pretend to be systematic or authoritative. Their sole aim has been to fix and record the fleeting sensations of the moment. Anything like a complete survey of the contemporary English stage would have been altogether beyond my purpose. I have been content to take the luck of the playbill, and so have often fallen upon banyan days. Hence one or two of our foremost dramatists are represented by plays which are certainly not their best. Others, whose names are placarded on the hoardings in the largest type, are not represented at all. Doubtless they have all, the popular and the unpopular, their several stations in the dramatic hierarchy; but it has been no affair of mine to "place" them. That is the function of judicial or dogmatic criticism—of which there are already, I submit, professors enough and to spare. The ideal critic is pictured by the crowd, now as a milestone "standing upon the antique ways," now as a finger-post on the " high priori" road. I have taken the less stately view of him as a vagabond, who accepts his impressions as they come, and changes his moods with his horizons. Hence, like other vagrom men, I have had an instinctive repugnance for the methods of the Bench. The enunciation of positive judgments, of absolute truths, I hold to be no part of my business: on the contrary, to be negative and relative was a point of honour. To have as many impressions as fortune willed—if irreconcilable, no matter—about the same work; to find the arguments for and against equally good; to be, in fine, multilateral, "*ondoyant et divers*"; these seemed to me the true objects of that "art of enjoying masterpieces," which is one sort of criticism. There are more imposing sorts, I know, the practitioners of which figure as the depositaries of eternal verities, as examiners distributing or refusing "testamurs," as official guardians of the public taste. One cannot, however, choose one's own temperament or one's own theory of criticism. It is to the lustre cast on it by M. Jules Lemaître that the "ondoyant" theory owes its charm for the present generation. I make no apology for the frequency with which that most brilliant of contemporary critics is cited in this volume. My only fear (for I cannot pretend to estimate in my own case the full extent of his influence) is lest I have not cited him often enough.

A. B. W.

CONTENTS.

	PAGE
PREFATORY NOTE	v
THE DRAMATIC CRITIC AS PARIAH	1
His Difficulties	7
He Bashkirtseffs	11
SHAKESPEARE—	
Much Ado	15
Hamlet	19
As You Like It	31
Taming of the Shrew	35
Antony and Cleopatra	42
HENRIK IBSEN—	
His Life	47
Rosmersholm	53
Hedda Gabler	59
Lady from the Sea	64
ALEXANDER THE GREATEST	68
DUMAS FILS	74
SARDOU	80
La Tosca	86
ALPHONSE DAUDET	92
JULES LEMAÎTRE	99
W. E. HENLEY AND R. L. STEVENSON	104
HENRY ARTHUR JONES—	
On Play-making	111
Middleman	116
Judah	119
The Realist in spite of himself	123
Dancing Girl	130

CONTENTS.

	PAGE
TERENCE, LABICHE, AND SYDNEY GRUNDY—	
Pair of Spectacles	135
Revisited	140
At Westminster	144
A. W. PINERO—	
Lady Bountiful	149
In Chancery	154
ROBERT BUCHANAN	157
J. K. JEROME—	
New Lamps for Old	163
Woodbarrow Farm	168
ARTIFICIAL COMEDY—	
Old Sherry	173
She Stoops to Conquer	177
London Assurance	185
THE OLD MELODRAMA—	
Belphegor	190
Formosa	193
THE NEW MELODRAMA—	
Idler	198
Diamond Deane	203
Fate and Fortune	208
BURLESQUE	212
PIERROTICS	218
THE ORPHEUS LEGEND—	
In Opera	225
In Ballet	229
THE HISTRIONIC TEMPERAMENT	234
SARAH BERNHARDT	239
CÉLINE CHAUMONT	245
COQUELIN AÎNÉ	251
HENRY IRVING	256

PLAYHOUSE IMPRESSIONS.

THE DRAMATIC CRITIC AS PARIAH.

A LITERARY Ishmael, he cannot choose but despond. His isolation is complete and tragic. From the people he criticises it were unreasonable to expect sympathy. His fellow playgoers regard him as a wet blanket. These "know what they like," and therefore look askance at the man whose function it is to convince them that they do not know what they ought to like. His natural kin, the serious intellects, treat him with good-humoured contempt. For he seems to them serious in the wrong place. He is perpetually asking for ideas on the stage, for recognition of the drama as a serious art. They openly prefer an unidea'd theatre and recognize the drama only as a frivolous pastime. "Probably there is nothing that serious intellects hate so much as 'an intellectual treat.' To be made to sit out a performance at the Français or the Lyceum would be to a great many of us an unmitigated bore. I believe high-class music, high-class plays, high-class novels are produced mainly for people of moderate or medium intelligence; people whose brains and bodies are systematically underworked. Men who have done a good day's toil with head or hands don't care for *Faust:* they want a Gaiety burlesque. The silliest song, the most rollicking fun, of the *cafés chantants* in the Champs Elysées or of the London Pavilion, is to many intelligent men a far greater relaxation than the best-mounted piece of Shakespeare's or Victor Hugo's. Or rather the one is a relaxation, and the other a nuisance."

These words of Mr. Grant Allen are noteworthy as the first appearance in print of a mental state, naked, and not ashamed, which is to be encountered at every dinner-table and in every smoking-room. They represent quite fairly, I am sure, the attitude towards the theatre of a large majority of the "serious intellects." The man who, for his sins, has to busy himself with dramatic criticism knows this attitude only too well. Let that man spend an evening—a privilege that sometimes falls to the lot even of such as he—in the society of university dons, men of science and the so-called learned professions. Then shall he learn what it is "to know his place." He will find himself treated like Mr. Gilbert's family fool, as a sort of buffoon to be joked with, dug in the ribs, importuned for orders (of which he is supposed to be a perpetual fount), or chaffed about fifteenth-rate actresses (of whom he is supposed to be the perpetual boon companion). That his occupation may be as serious, and as seriously undertaken, as that of any of his fellow guests, never enters their heads They regard him as lightly as they would the ingenious gentleman at the Alhambra who spins plates on the end of his nose. That the drama is an art, like another, with a good to be encouraged and a bad to be eschewed, is no creed of theirs. What their creed is, Mr. Grant Allen plainly tells us. We "serious intellects" are only serious in the study; in the theatre we become Philistines. Where the drama is concerned we have no taste, and we are not ashamed to say so.

It is the unhesitating acceptance of this strange creed by many otherwise thoughtful young Englishmen that one has to reckon among the rocks ahead of the reviving English drama. The fatal truth is, that the "serious intellect" is in England an intellect cultivated at the expense of its owner's taste. The archetype is Darwin—Darwin who tells us he detested Shakespeare and could read nothing but trashy novels from Mudie's. Mr. Grant Allen—in high repute as the exponent of popular Darwinism, the apostle of Darwinism to the Gentiles—is thus only following in the footsteps of the Master. The way in which people of this type regard the drama was significantly shown when Mr. William Archer published his "Masks or Faces?" This book, which was remarkable as being the first really scientific investigation (in English) of the psychology of histrionics, was entrusted for review —one would have thought, fitly—by a certain editor to a certain man of science. What said our reviewer? Did he rejoice that the true scientific method had at length invaded the literature of the stage—a region hitherto laid waste by the flashy anecdote-monger and the shallow empiricist? Not he. He only acknowledged the scientific spirit of the book in order to complain that it should have been thrown away on such a trashy subject. What does it matter, he argued in effect, whether actors do or do not feel their parts? What interest can "serious intellects" take in a matter so piffling? Yet this piffling matter had not been thought beneath the grave consideration of such "serious intellects" as Diderot, as Lessing, as Dr. Johnson, and as Mr. John Morley.

And thus it befal's that, thanks to the spirit represented by gentlemen like this scientific reviewer, or like Mr. Grant Allen and his friends, you now have the Français and Lyceum occupied by "people of moderate or medium intelligence," and that if you want to find the real head-workers, the "serious intellects," you must seek them at the Gaiety and the Pavilion. There is a grim humour about this assertion that reminds one of the biting sarcasms of the Abbé who took Candide to the play. But the case of my friend Crito convinces me that Mr. Grant Allen's statement, at any rate so far as the second half of it is concerned, is quite correct. Crito took a Double First, the Hertford, the Craven, and a Balliol Fellowship before he was five-and-twenty. He is now a high official at the Museum, will some day be Deputy-Sub-Assistant-Librarian, and is meanwhile the most brilliant of University Extension Lecturers. His monograph on Court Sinecures under the Heptarchy, and his famous essay proving that Junius was not Junius, but another man of the same name, have been translated into every known language. In pure scholarship he out-Bentleys Bentley, and is more Porsonian than Porson. In short, I don't know a more "serious intellect" than Crito's. Crito sometimes spends an evening at the play, sometimes at those halls which, according to the County Council (evidently composed of "serious intellects"), are alone entitled to be considered places of entertainment. Whom do you take to be Crito's favourite artists? Salvini, Bernhardt, Coquelin, Ellen Terry? No—Mr. Arthur Roberts and Miss Elizabeth Bellwood. He once went to the Lyceum, and that was with a complimentary ticket; but he went six times to see the *pas de quatre* in *Faust up to Date*, and was a constant attendant at *Ruy Blas, or the Blasé Roué*. Now, without discussing, for the moment, the entertainment provided at our burlesque theatres, one may be pardoned for thinking that Crito, by confining his patronage to that particular kind of entertainment, is helping to play the deuce with the prospects of the modern stage. He is—to steal a bit of George Eliot's phrase — helping to debase the dramatic currency.

Crito is bad enough, but I think another friend of mine, Euthyphro, is worse. Euthyphro hardly falls into Mr. Grant Allen's category of "serious intellects," for none has ever known him to be serious, but about his intellect there is, as the Grand Inquisitor says—

> No probable possible shadow of doubt,
> No possible doubt whatever.

A universal genius, a brilliant political economist, a Fabian of the straitest sect of the Fabians, a critic (of other arts than the dramatic) *comme il y en a peu*, he persists, where the stage is concerned, in crying for the moon, and will not be satisfied, as the rest of us have learned to be, with the only attainable substitute, a good wholesome cheese. His standard of taste is as much too high as Crito's is too low. He asks from the theatre more than the theatre can give, and quarrels with the theatre because it is theatrical. He lumps *La Tosca* and *A Man's Shadow* together as "French machine-made plays," and, because he is not edified by them, refuses to be merely amused. Because *The Dead Heart* is not on the level of a Greek tragedy, he is blind to its merits as a pantomime. He refuses to recognize the advance made by Mr. Pinero, because Mr. Pinero has not yet advanced as far as Henrik Ibsen. Half a loaf, the wise agree, is better than no bread; but because it is only half a loaf, Euthyphro complains that they have given him a stone. And the worst of it is, Euthyphro is a man of influence. He is a prophet in Israel. Many more or less "serious intellects," who have only the vaguest notion of what Euthyphro is driving at, are yet content to take their cue from him. They have never been to the play, but Euthyphro is for them " the man who has been there, don't you know, and ought to know." So they take his opinion on trust—and stay away.

HIS DIFFICULTIES.

DESPISED by the "serious intellects," the critic turns in vain to the actor. Actors are notoriously shy of critics, because critics wear shocking bad hats; but there are exceptions to every rule, and there is one affable comedian who has consented to overlook my hat. Still, somehow, what is under the bad hats doesn't quite satisfy him. His grievance against the critics is that they should produce so much elaborate criticism of plays and playwrights, and so little serviceable criticism of players. Why, he asks, are the public treated to whole columns about the piece, and only to a couple of "sticks" about the acting? Gentlemen of the Press are very fond of teaching the playwrights how to write plays, why don't they tell the actors how to act?

In his last question my friend has fallen into the not uncommon error of supposing criticism to be a didactic art; but there is, perhaps, something in his grievance. There is of dramatic criticism enough and to spare; but there is little, if any, genuine criticism of histrionics. The actors think this is only a part of the general "cussedness" of their natural enemies, the critics. But let us try to be more sweetly reasonable than the actors, and see if we cannot find a subtler explanation. My first reason may seem whimsical to the matter-of-fact outsider, but all professional scribblers will, I believe, recognize it as a true one. Your critic is a sedentary person with the literary bias. His instinct is to bring to a play the calm lotos-eating mood with which he day-dreams over a book in his library. To this frame of mind the boisterous flesh-and-blood element of the actors comes as a rude distraction. Oxford, said the cynic, would be a delightful place if it were empty of Oxford men; the playhouse, the literary critic feels in his heart of hearts, would be a pleasant place without the players. Here you touch a paradox of the acted drama: the very means that make it possible to judge of it hinder judgment. Of this type of critic Hazlitt is the great example. "The players," Talfourd records, "put him out." Secondly, the critic is tempted to shirk speaking of the actors from a natural delicacy. It is the peculiarity of the actor's art that his artistic materials are composed of his own physical personality. He himself is his own paint and canvas. Hence observations on his acting are bound to verge upon the dangerous ground of "personal remarks." Now it irks a gentleman who is probably no Adonis himself (thank goodness, his calling doesn't require that of him!) to have to discuss the tilt of another gentleman's nose. When ladies are concerned, the critic's distress is, of course, much more poignant. I shudder as I think of some fair lady pointing me out to a sister-actress. "Do you see that sandy, pock-marked little fellow over there in the bad hat? He had the impudence to say of me the other day, that 'I was a tolerable Doll Tearsheet; but that my Juliet lacked the indefinable quality known as charm.' Now, what can a horrid little wretch like that know about charm?" So the critic naturally prefers to talk about the play, which has no feelings to be hurt.

My thirdly is deducible from the preceding reason.

If " personal remarks " have to be made, there is a tendency to make them agreeable to their subject, and compliments are not criticism. I well remember the advice once given me by the dramatic critic *en titre* of a certain old-fashioned newspaper. "My boy, your discussions of the Three Unities, your long quotations from Aristotle in the original Greek, your parallels between G. R. Sims and Lope de Vega, are ingenious and scholarly, and all that; but the public don't understand 'em, and our sub-editor has orders to cut 'em out. Write something the actors can quote. Always have a good quotable paragraph." And now, as I run my eye down the Press notices in the morning papers, I flatter myself I can generally spot the "quotable paragraph." Next day out it comes in the advertisement columns—you know the sort of thing.

FRIVOLITY THEATRE.—GIGANTIC SUCCESS.

The Daily Gazette says :—
"Cheered to the echo."

The Mercury says :—
"Will draw all London to the historic little house in Queer-street."

The Morning Mail says :—
"The most monumental of all Mr. Vincent Crummles' colossal creations. Veteran playgoers who had been in the pit that 'rose at' Kean, or who had shuddered with awe at Sarah Siddons, wept like children. The whole house one sob," &c., &c.

Another reason why some writers abstain from serious criticism of actors is peculiar to journalism— or was, for even in the most old-fashioned quarters one would not, I suppose, find an editor nowadays instructing his dramatic critic as Delane instructed John Oxenford. An actor whom Oxenford had sharply criticised (the story is told by Mr. Edmund Yates) complained in a strong letter to the editor. "I have no doubt you were perfectly right in all you wrote," said Delane to his critic, "but that is not the question. Whether a man acts well or ill is of very little consequence to the great body of our readers, and I could not think of letting the paper become the field for argument on the point. So, in future, you understand, my good fellow, write your notices so as much as possible to avoid this sort of letter being addressed to the office." And, finally, criticism of acting is shirked because of the critics' lack of technical knowledge. This is not their fault. They are not actors; and how can they be acquainted with even the rudiments of histrionics, when no one will teach them? There is no Conservatoire in London where the conscientious critic could attend a course of lectures, if he would; actors give lessons to would-be actors, but who ever heard of an actor offering to instruct a would-be critic? Our actors and actresses print their reminiscences, or their impressions of foreign travel, or their ideas about plays (which is the critic's affair and not theirs); but plain elementary instruction about their own business—the art of acting—they cannot be induced to print.

HE BASHKIRTSEFFS.

THUS isolated, the critic—it is the common fate of all "solitaries"—is driven in upon himself, becomes a self-tormentor, at best a self-revealer. And so I do not wonder that a dramatist of my acquaintance who has done me the honour to glance at these my poor lucubrations complains that they are too autobiographical. He finds that the subjective is to the objective in them too often in the inordinate proportion of sack to bread in Falstaff's tavern bill. Another acquaintance—a ribald fellow this one, an 'ακόλαστος, a lewd fellow of the baser sort—puts the same complaint in the form of a fable. I have exhausted, he affirms, the whole stock of capital I's at the printers, and they had to send out in hot haste for a fresh supply. Yet another acquaintance (a Scotchman, with the literal mind of his race) suggests that, to carry my principles of "impressionist" criticism to their logical conclusion, I ought to head this article with the *menu* of the dinner I have eaten before writing it. It is unnecessary for me to add that this person cultivates literature on a little oatmeal and Salutaris water.

In vain have I laboured to convince these assailants that all criticism, rightly considered, *is* autobiography. They will not be persuaded, and their gibes —shall I confess it?—have left me a little shamefaced, a little despondent. I have even gone over my "copy" and tried to substitute for the capital I's "nouns of multitude signifying many," or some of those well-worn stereotypes—"it is thought," "one may be pardoned for hinting," "will any one deny?" &c., &c.—by which criticism keeps up the pretence that it is not a man but a corporation. Fortunately, the imposture of the thing has been too much for my powers; naturally fond of lying as I am, and as all healthy-minded men are—for this particular kind of lie I have no talent. Still I was for a while despondent.

But now I am comforted. The good Samaritan who has poured in oil and wine is M. Anatole France, and he has done it in a sentence which puts the whole theory of autobiographical criticism in a nutshell. "The good critic is he who narrates the adventures of his soul among masterpieces." Thus I steal my *apologia*, as the youngster stole his brooms, ready-made. True, there is a little hitch about the "masterpieces." Masterpieces do not encounter the dramatic critic so often as might be wished. But that is not my fault. I supply the "soul" and the "adventures" (or, if you like, "misadventures"). I have executed my share of the contract. Some reader asks: Who is M. Anatole France? Happy reader! If he does not know M. Anatole France there is a charming friendship awaiting him. Go to Mudie's and ask for "Le Crime de Sylvestre Bonnard." It is a simple story and a bloodless. There are no South American savages in it, no Umslopogaases, no tribes who crown other tribes with red-hot iron pots. An old bachelor bookworm becomes interested in an orphan whose mother he had once loved, he helps her to run away from the school where she is ill-treated, and marries her to a young scientific man. That is all; but that "all" is literature. M. Anatole France is, however, something more (and, as I have the temerity to think, something better) than a fine novelist. He is a fine critic. Under the title of "La Vie Littéraire" (Paris: Calmann Lévy) he has issued a collection of what Sainte-Beuve and Mr. Pater would call "appreciations," and it is therein I find my comforting sentence about autobiographic criticism.

I cannot deny myself the pleasure of transcribing the rest of the passage. "There is no objective criticism any more than there is objective art, and all those who flatter themselves that they put something else than themselves into their work are dupes of the cheapest illusion. The truth is, we never get out of ourselves. That is one of our greatest miseries. What would we not give to see, for one minute, heaven and earth with the facetted eye of a fly, or to comprehend Nature with the rude and simple brain of an ourang-outang? But that is denied to us. We cannot, like Tiresias, be a man and yet remember we have been a woman. We are shut up in our own person as in some perpetual prison-house. The best thing we can do, it seems to me, is to recognize this frightful limitation with a good grace and to confess that we are speaking of ourselves—whenever we have not the strength to hold our tongues. To be frank, the critic should say, 'Gentlemen, I am going to talk about myself *àpropos* of Shakespeare, or of Goethe. Could I have a better opportunity?'" It is time we heard the last of this stale complaint against people for talking about themselves. After all, there is no subject they can treat better, for there is none which interests them so much. The worthy souls who were so angry with George Eliot for declaring that her favourite book was "Rousseau's Confessions" must have been egregious dullards. Let them ponder over the popularity of the Diary of Marie Bashkirtseff. I can fancy some one objecting that the value of autobiography depends upon the autobiographer. Egoistic literature, by all means, provided that the egoist is a genius like Rousseau or an orchidaceous personality like Marie Bashkirtseff. But you must be something out of the common before you have the right to talk about what you are. The egoism that is not wanted is the egoism of mediocrity, the egoism, say, of a mere theatrical critic.

Granting (just for the sake of argument) that a critic can be mediocre, I still decline to admit this contention. Who was the sage who said that if any plain citizen, the man in the street, were to set down day by day with absolute sincerity his thoughts and actions he would produce the most fascinating book ever written? There is much to admire (the only reflection that prevents me from opening my veins in a bath) in an ordinary person. Not to mention that what we admire in him we rediscover in ourselves, a thing always pleasant. Sing hey! then, for autobiography in criticism. It is the great critic's crowning glory and the poor criticaster's saving grace. The charm of a Hazlitt and a De Quincey, it serves to excuse the humblest of us, so long as he shall be sincere. There is a special reason for its existence in dramatic criticism, where it represents a reaction against the absolute impersonality of the drama, the one form of literature from which egoism is rigorously banished. It is (in another sense than that of the metaphysicians) the Ego reasserting itself against the Non-Ego.

SHAKESPEARE.

"MUCH ADO ABOUT NOTHING."

(*Lyceum Theatre, January*, 1891.)

"HEY, nonny, nonny." The revival of *Much Ado About Nothing* at the Lyceum has sent us all back once more to the enchanting and enchanted Messina of Shakespeare, that strange far-off Messina of the Italian Renaissance which is a table-land above the Delectable Mountains and yet is among the Happy Isles, which marches on the one side with Bohemia-by-the-Sea and on the other with the Kingdom of the Coqcigrues. Here full-blooded, nimble-witted, sixteenth-century gallants, full of the New Learning as of the Old Adam, as ready with their *concetti* as with their poniards, play hide-and-seek behind visor or in cedar-sheltered pleasaunces with stately Titian damsels whose tirewomen have anticipated Lothair's "ropes of pearls," while English watchmen slouch sleepily through the throng, and as unconcernedly as though Messina were in the heart of their own Warwickshire. "Hey, nonny, nonny." What is the peculiar charm of this piece? How shall one analyze it? The first and, I think, the dominant impression is an impression of intense vitality, of *la joie de vivre*, or (to be in the latest fashion) of the Schopenhauerian Will to Live. They are all so very much alive, these swaggering gentlemen and gorgeous ladies, all, as Leonato says, in the "May of youth and bloom of lustihood." Ay, even the greybeards (Act v. sc. 2). So much alive that they go a-courting at the very foot of the high altar (Act iv.), amid organ-peals and fumes of frankincense. So much alive that even when they have, or think they have, done innocent brides to death, they are yet ready with heartless quip and crank for bereaved fathers (Claudio, Act v. sc. 2). And the women, mark you, no less than the men. "No glory lives behind the back of maiden pride" for them (Act iii. sc. 1). Beatrice, as Margaret thinks (Act v. sc. 2), "hath legs." So have they all, and are not ashamed of it. They are no Queens of Spain. That is one's first impression, an impression of life. The second is that this life is the peculiar life of the Renaissance. They are all great readers. Even the women have probably studied Plato with Roger Ascham. Beatrice, at any rate, has read the "Hundred Merry Tales" (Act i. sc. 3). The men are choke-full of the classic lore of the new time, a time—

"Sentant encor le lait dont elle fut nourrie."

Benedick talks glibly of Leander and Troilus (Act v. sc. 2), and writes verse—bad verse, as a scholar-soldier should—"a *halting* sonnet of his own poor brain" (Act v. sc. 4). Claudio is a bard. Part of his penance, if you please, for killing a poor lady is to "hang her an epitaph upon her tomb, and sing it to her bones" (Act v. sc. 2). But life and letters do not sum up the Renaissance; they must be completed by a touch of the lurid—Benvenuto Cellini must cut Pompeo's throat, as well as carve in silver—and so we get our third impression. This is an impression of sombre melodrama, Italian treachery, the intrusion of Mephistopheles into the *Kermesse* which the dramatist has provided for us in the intrigue of Don John and Borachio. Mr. Irving's restoration of this element of the story, an element almost ignored in previous stage-practice, is an example of the sound judgment he seldom fails to show in such matters. In France (where the play was adapted a few years ago by M. Louis Legendre for the Odéon) they have carried this restoration a step farther by representing on the stage the scene between Borachio and Margaret at the window, which Shakespeare has been content merely to narrate—an instance, most Englishmen will think, of zeal in excess. Can I register a fourth impression? Yes; in the strange manner of Claudio's wooing—behind a mask and in the person of his prince—I like to fancy a premonition of the theatre of Hugo and Musset. And when Claudio consents to wed a veiled lady whom he has never seen, he is the direct ancestor of Don César de Bazan. Thus are the Elizabethan and the Romantic epoch brought together. One might go on to a fifthly or a fifteenthly —all merging at last into one composite picture of the multifarious, seething, fermenting life, the polychromatic phantasmagoria of the Renaissance. Like some quaint book of the time, with a quainter title, some "Hypnerotomachia Poliphili," or like some vast crowded canvas of the time—that great marriage-piece, say, of Veronese in the Salon Carré of the Louvre—*Much Ado about Nothing* is an Inn of Strange Meetings.

My excuse for dwelling upon this aspect of the piece rather than upon the "merry war" of Beatrice and Benedick is, that the latter topic is by this time more than a little stale. There is nothing new to be said about it, unless one adopts M. Jules Lemaître's shocking heresy, and calls the pair of combatants "insupportable—savages trying to be witty—extremely subtle brutes." Any Englishman who ventured on that would ever afterwards require a police-escort, so I forbear. "Hey, nonny, nonny."

"HAMLET."

(A Bookman's View.)

I OPEN "Short Studies of Shakespeare's Plots," by Cyril Ransome, M.A.—Mr. Ransome is a professor of modern literature in one of the new north-country universities, whose lectures on Shakespeare to popular audiences have been published in book form—and on the very first page I find a split infinitive: "to carefully banish." Overleaf occurs the expression, "a threefold alternative"; a little further on comes the sentence, "Which of these views, *or either*, is right": the Hot Gospeller's vulgarism, "humanly speaking," crops up more than once; and the opening chapter yields the infelicitous misquotation, "*Old* saws and modern instances." All these little matters, trifling enough in themselves, cease to be so when they convict a university professor of slipshod English and a Shakespearean commentator of ignorance, not merely of the most hackneyed speech in Shakespeare, but of the Elizabethan use of the word "modern."

But it would be a waste of time to test the Professor's book by the methods of what Mr. Saintsbury calls the mint and anise and cummin school of criticism. It is, indeed, as a protest against such criticism in the case of Shakespeare that his book, he tells us, is primarily intended. He complains, very justly, of the usual school teaching of Shakespeare as mere word-splitting. Beginners are too often taught to read Shakespeare rather as a vocabulary of strange idioms than as a masterpiece of literature, because, as the Professor shrewdly observes, examiners find philological knowledge the easiest to mark. He might have added: because the examiners themselves have, as a rule, no other knowledge of the subject. The Professor now comes to the rescue of the philology-ridden student with what he considers a new method. This is no other than the scientific method, the method of observation, "the same method as that which has unfolded the secrets of the natural world." The Professor's intentions, at any rate, are excellent. A proposed "scientific" study of Shakespeare has a fine seductiveness for the serious student. Let us see how the new method is to be applied. In the first place, then, we are to banish from our minds all preconceived notions about the plays, all theories of Shakespeare's mind or art. Then we are to forget any representation of a Shakespearean play at which we have been present (Heavens! As far as most of them go, one wishes one could!). And now, with our mind a perfect *tabula rasa*, we are to examine the text, act by act, scene by scene, and nothing but the text. "To do this is to throw upon Shakespeare his full responsibility as a literary artist. Neither acting nor scenery will serve his turn with us. What he has to say he must say himself, and we may be sure that, if we have the wit to see it, we shall find in the text the key to every problem which the story may suggest." I fancy I can hear the roars of indulgent laughter which this contention would have provoked from the company at the Mermaid. As if that part of literature which is called drama could be properly judged without reference to the conditions of the very object with which it is written! As if the whole structure of a play were not dependent on the fact that it is to be acted! The text of a play is no more the play than a score is music. According to this astonishing contention, to read the pianoforte arrangement of the "Eroica" Symphony is to throw upon Beethoven his full responsibility as a musical artist.

But let us, for the moment, take the Professor at his word, and follow him in the application of his method to *Hamlet*. I choose *Hamlet*, as the play most favourable to the Professor's case. Every play addresses itself to much more than the intellect: it imparts sensations much more than ideas: it propagates waves of emotion, kindles sympathy or antipathy much more than it appeals to the logical faculty. Hence any merely intellectual analysis of a play is foredoomed to failure. But it fails less in *Hamlet*—the most intellectual of all Shakespeare's plays—than in any other. We are, then, to take *Hamlet* scene by scene, and to ask ourselves at every pause—1. What has this scene done to advance the story? 2. What light has been thrown by it upon the character of the persons concerned?

Now, one of the very first reflections which any unbiassed reader is bound to make about *Hamlet* is that the play abounds in long-winded speeches, of which the common characteristic is that they jump *from the particular to the general.* They may not be exactly out of key with the character, or altogether useless to the action, but, at first sight at any rate, they do appear as somewhat disproportionate to the dramatic exigencies of the situation. Hamlet himself never once lets the opportunity slip for moralizing at large. He goes out on the platform at Elsinore to interview the ghost. We are all a tip-toe with expectation, all eager, as M. Sarcey would say, for the *scène-à-faire*. But some one unfortunately drops an observation about the King keeping "wassail," and so we have to wait for our *scène-à-faire* while Hamlet moralizes upon the general weakness of humanity for strong ale, as though he were addressing a temperance crowd at the Crystal Palace, instead of waiting in an exposed situation on a cold, windy night for an unpunctual ghost. He cannot welcome a company of strolling players without delivering a lecture (extremely valuable, but quite uncalled for at the moment) on histrionics. If he meditates on suicide (in the absurdly overrated "To be or not to be" farrago) he must need drag in, not merely his own woes, but those with which (*e.g.*, "law's delay"!) he can only have had a hearsay acquaintance. Always, observe, the jump is *from the particular to the general*. Hamlet is not the only offender. In the words of Lady Regula Baddun's favourite ballad, they all do it. Polonius cannot see his son off to Paris without delivering a long string of Prud'hommesque maxims on the art of life. Laertes is just as bad. He cannot say *au revoir* to his sister without a whole budget of vague generalizations about princes' love and maidens' modesty.

How are these speeches accounted for on the Professor's text-and-nothing-but-the-text principles? In the text, remember, "we shall find the key to every problem." The Professor, like the characters in *Dr. Bill*, is always on the hunt for the key. He won't be happy till he gets it. Unfortunately he is driven to getting it by the process known to the French as "seeking noon at fourteen o'clock"—the fate of all commentators who regard a Shakespearean play as a sort of machine for grinding out logic. Witness Coleridge. To explain the apparent incongruity of placing Polonius's homily on conduct in the mouth of a comic character, Coleridge starts the theory that Polonius is *not* a comic character. Professor Ransome "goes one better" than Coleridge. For him Polonius and Laertes are intended to illustrate the law of heredity. "Polonius is the true father of Laertes. As a young man he has had the same trick of lecturing his friends as Laertes has now, and it has grown upon him. His loquaciousness has increased with his years." And Shakespeare's making the old fool talk wisdom is only a subtle stroke of irony. "All (*i.e.*, Polonius's maxims) are made singularly humorous by the contrast they bear to the subsequent conduct of their utterer." To account for Hamlet's superfluous moralizings the Professor might, of course, take refuge in the safe, if conventional, position that they serve to illustrate his character, of which the essence is a nature that "unpacks itself with words." But that is not ingenious enough for a gentleman with a brand-new method. Accordingly we are told that Hamlet is made to speak the speech to the players "to guard against the audience falling into the mistake that Hamlet was mad." In the moralizing over Yorick's skull we are asked to see Shakespeare's irony once more at work. "The reflections Hamlet offers on the uncertainty of life afford the best satire upon the use he is making of it." But it is when confronted by Hamlet's "wassail" speech in the first act that the new criticism "exposes" (in the immortal phrase of the Calcutto baboo) "its *cui bono* in all its native hideousness." Coleridge found in this practically irrelevant speech an attempt on Hamlet's part to "smother the impatience of the moment in abstract reasoning." Professor Ransome feels that a supreme effort of exegesis is here demanded of him. "This speech of Hamlet's requires careful study. It is introduced by Shakespeare apparently without need, *and therefore it must have been* designed by him either to give some important information about Hamlet's own character, or to supply the audience with some caution or hint which would aid them in understanding the play."

At last the cat is out of the bag! We are not only, it now appears, to ask our two questions after each speech, how far, namely, has it (1) furthered the progress of the story, (2) illustrated the character of the speaker; but we are to assume that it was necessarily intended by the author to do one or the other, or both. Here is the Professor fallen a victim to the very danger he began by warning us against—a preconceived theory of Shakespeare's art ! The theory is sound enough in contemporary dramatic criticism. It is by this theory that we assign to Ibsen his pre-eminent rank ; it is by this theory we condemn the "purple patches" of Dumas *fils*. But to apply it to the Elizabethan stage is to show a deplorable forgetfulness of the law of evolution in literature. Nowadays we expect a drama to be purely dramatic. " Specialization of function " (as Professor Ransome has appealed to science, to science he must go) has done its work. But it ought not to be necessary to remind a Professor of Modern Literature that in the sixteenth century the drama had not yet been clearly differentiated from other literary forms. Say rather that it as yet combined them all. It had much of the epic (the "chronicle plays"), still more of the lyric (the "pastorals" and the "fairy plays"); and it contained in large measure (*Hamlet* is the great example) that element of mixed philosophy and rhetoric which was soon afterwards to be diverted into other channels, in England by Sir Thomas

Browne, in France by the great pulpit orators. The existence of the last element was greatly fostered (and here is a little fact which no amount of text-and-nothing-but-the-text study would ever reveal) by the merely mechanical conditions of the stage, which (a glance at any authentic print of an Elizabethan theatre will show why) made Elizabethan acting quite as much a rhetorical as an imitative art. These facts are trite and patent to all students of Shakespeare, except to those who obstinately shut their eyes to everything but the text—and they give the key to those *Hamlet* speeches which have prompted Professor Ransome and Coleridge and many other excellent persons to attempt their unnecessary feats of intellectual gymnastics. Such speeches as the homily of Polonius, or Hamlet's lecture to the players, were not designed by Shakespeare to further the action or to illustrate character, nor were they for one moment so regarded by the Elizabethan man in the pit. Shakespeare simply wanted to philosophize about life or the drama, the man in the pit wanted to hear about these things, and when both of them got their chance neither cared a hang about Professor Ransome's pet test-questions. The moral of the Professor's book (notwithstanding that it contains many fresh and wise things and much really luminous criticism) is : Study Shakespeare by the text alone, and you will assuredly find mares' nests.

"HAMLET."

(*Globe Theatre, March, 1890.*)

IL me faut aujourd hui parler d'Hamlet; c'est horrible. By these words, with which M. Jules Lemaître opens one of his *feuilletons*, he does not mean that the play is horrible ; what inspires the critic with horror is the necessity of having to discourse on a subject about which everything—and more—has already been a thousand times said. It is impossible for the truest of true-born Englishmen not to be in sympathy on this point with the darned mounseer. In the jargon of the studios, *Hamlet* is undoubtedly "an old hat " ; it is to the dramatic critic what the Thames at Streatley or the Grand Canal at Venice is to the painter ; there is no point of view from which it has not been done, re-done, and overdone. Needs must, however, when the devil drives. Mr. Benson has produced *Hamlet* at the Globe, and, willy-nilly, something has to be said about the production by the critic. But, as M. Lemaître groans, *c'est horrible.*

For my part, I have kept *Hamlet* under lock and key in my library (in the secret recess where Captain Burton's "Arabian Nights," the novels of Rétif de la Bretonne, the Memoirs of Casanova, and other works unsuited for family reading lie hidden) ever since the recent publication of a book entitled "God in Shakespeare," by one "Clelia." This Clelia attacked the "To be or not to be" soliloquy, and gave it an entirely new misinterpretation by substituting, somewhere or other, a colon (:) for a note of interrogation (?). For Clelia "this colon (:) was a brilliant core of light, darting its rays in all directions, rolling back doubt and darkness." For me it made life intolerable. "To sleep, perchance to dream"—about this darting and rolling colon (:)—was henceforth a nightly terror. So, when Mr. Benson began "To be, or not to be," I just stopped my ears and hummed a stave of "It's another colour now," till the pit cried "S-h-h!" Why, by the by, does the pit cry "S-h-h!" so boldly? It allows itself every kind of licence, especially in the way of coughing, nose-blowing, and feet-shuffling. Yet a poor critic in the stalls may not relieve his feelings by a scrap from the joyous repertory of the Music Halls without—but this is a digression. Will any one tell me why Mr. Benson revived *Hamlet* at the Globe? It is so easy, said the French cynic, not to write a tragedy in five acts. It is so easy, one would have thought, not to revive *Hamlet*. Yet all would-be Shakespearean actors do it. Is the reason to be found in the pet remark of Macready—he repeats it at least half a dozen times in his Diary—that no actor has ever yet been known to fail as Hamlet? But, on the other hand, has any actor been known completely to succeed? Of recent years we Londoners have had Mr. Irving's Hamlet, which was Irvingesque; we have had Mr. Edwin Booth's Hamlet, full of such new readings as "haff a yeer" and other transatlantic delights; we have had Mr. Wilson Barrett's Hamlet, the ideal Hamlet, it has been said, of the British vestryman—a ten-pound householder Hamlet. In Paris they have had the shrieking and scolding Hamlet of M. Marais, and the whining lachrymose Hamlet of M. Mounet Sully. But has any one of these Hamlet's been a success? Has any one of them been Shakespeare's Hamlet? Have you any idea what Shakespeare's Hamlet was? Here's a pretty string of questions! But I can't help putting my remarks interrogatively: 'tis the result of seeing *Hamlet* at the Globe. Is not Hamlet himself one prolonged query?

To pass, however, from questions to answers, it seems to me that *Hamlet* holds the stage because, like the omnibus of everyday life, it has an inside and an outside, and because, again, like the omnibus (under the present dispensation of "garden-seats"), the outside is by far the more attractive division of the two. By the outside I mean the mere story-telling element of the play, its action apart from its poetry and psychology. This is rapid, bustling, romantic, and yet not improbable. Indeed, I have a theory that were Hamlet himself a mere dummy, a walking-gentleman with all his soliloquies cut out, the action in which he takes part would still make a fairly exciting play. In other words, the play of *Hamlet* with the part of Hamlet left out—a notion which has become a common mock and by-word— might conceivably be very good fun. Suppose, for instance, Mr. Walter Pollock were to treat it as he has treated Watts Phillips's *Dead Heart*, keeping only just so much of the dialogue as is needed to carry the incidents along? The experiment is at least worth trying. Just modernize the story a bit, and you will see what I mean. Why, you might come across it any day in the news columns of the evening papers, cross-headings and all!

"SHOCKING AFFAIR IN OHIO—A SPIRITUALIST GOES MAD, AND MURDERS A WHOLE FAMILY.

"The American papers are full of a tragic story from Ohio. A young Harvard student, Silas P. Hamlet, whose mother, Gertrude, had married her deceased husband's brother, Colonel the Hon. Z. Claudius, had fallen a victim to the wiles of the spirit-rapping fraternity, by whom he was deluded into believing that his late father, Judge Hamlet, had been

POISONED BY THE COLONEL.

This delusion, coupled with the young man's conscientious objection to marriage-with-a-deceased-husband's-brother, so worked upon his mind that he "guyed" his stepfather, the colonel, in some private theatricals, and shot Old Brer Polonius, the faithful coloured servant of the family, whom he found airing his eye

AT THE KEYHOLE.

For this offence he had to get away for a time to Texas, but, returning unexpectedly, forced Artemus W. Laertes, one of the best leaders of the "German" in Ohio, into a duel with rifles. Both combatants perished, but not until the colonel had been shot by his stepson, and his lady had been accidentally poisoned by drinking from a bottle of liniment that had been brought on the ground. The leading citizens have subscribed to give the family a first-class funeral."

There! You cannot deny that would make an exciting play. And now you see why *Hamlet* still holds the stage. But, even as it is, the elder Alexandre Dumas thought it might be made more exciting. So (somewhere in the Forties) here∙wrote the fifth act, reintroducing the Ghost, who pronounces death upon all in turn thus:—

> (*To Laertes*) Prie et meurs !
>   (*Laerte meurt.*)
> (*To Gertrude*) Espère et meurs !
>   (*Gertrude meurt.*)
> (*To the King*) Desespère et meurs !
>   (*Le roi meurt.*)

— but keeps Hamlet for further use with the announcement,
    Tu vivras !

"AS YOU LIKE IT."

(Lyceum Theatre, July, 1890.)

SO infinite is the variety of the impressions one gets from *As You Like It*, so wide their range, that it is a hopeless adventure to classify and label them. Once you have peeped through the leaves of the enchanted forest, you see all the kingdoms of the world of thought spread out before you, but no ordnance surveyor can map that country to scale. "There we stare with amazed eyes," says Heine of 'the magic garden of Shakespearean comedy,' "and see how lords and ladies, shepherds and shepherdesses, fools and sages, wander about under the tall trees; how the lover and his loved one rest in the cool shadows and exchange tender words; how, now and then, a fabulous animal, perhaps a stag with silver horns, comes by, or else a chaste unicorn, leaping from the thicket, lays his head in the lovely lady's lap." Yes, we stare with amazed eyes. Still, in the welter of one's impressions, some one must surge to the surface and overtop the rest: and if you ask me what that dominant impression ought to be, after a good and true representation of *As You Like It*, I would say, "Did it hypnotise you?" Applying this test to Miss Ada Rehan's performance, I find it beyond all cavil good and true. It hypnotised me. I walked out of the Lyceum in a trance, thinking that the very "growlers" in the Strand must be so named after the lions in Arden, and that the unwashed ruffian who yelled "Keb or kerridge, sir," was really a "A country fellow in love with Audrey," disguised. Then came along a Devil's Advocate and linked his arm in mine.

"Ada Rehan's Rosalind is not for my market," said the fellow. "A bouncing Rosalind! Not half enough refinement for a duke's daughter! Always steeplechasing about the stage! Did you notice what a business she made over covering her legs in the 'Alack! my doublet and hose!' passage? Made as much fuss as though she had been Susannah surprised by the Elders! In fact, the whole thing was overdone."

Thus the Devil's Advocate. He little knew what it is to throw the cold douche of ratiocination over a hypnotised patient. At the corner of Villiers Street I gave him in charge for trying to rob me of a dream, and as he was hustled away in handcuffs I could hear him trying to explain to policeman X Y Z his hideous common-sense views about bouncing Rosalinds.

The deuce of it was, that there was a certain leaven of truth in what the fellow said. Miss Rehan's Rosalind certainly cannot be said to err on the side of under-playing. They have a saying on the Isis that one 'Varsity oar is enough to ruin a college eight, and the remark is not without its bearing on the question of playing *As You Like It*.

The stronger the player's personality the more one feels, if fastidiously minded, the unwelcome intrusion of a solid body between the Shakespearean phantasmagoria and one's self. Stendhal was once asked whether he had ever seen Shakespeare perfectly acted. "Yes, once," he answered, "by a set of mediocre players, in a barn." And there are those who still think, with Stendhal, that mediocre players serve best for *As You Like It*, players who only suggest what the playgoer's fancy shall fill in, instead of really great players, whose personality overpowers and gets in the way. And so Théophile Gautier in the ideal performance of this play, which he sketches out in "Mademoiselle de Maupin," has it acted by well-bred amateurs. To such minds, in such moods, Miss Rehan must seem to overact Rosalind.

But not to me, who have been hypnotised. On cool reflection, I quite admit the blemishes. She is certainly too restless. In the mock-courting scenes with Orlando she must cover a distance that, measured by a pedometer, would probably tot up to a respectable figure. Perhaps, too, she does forget to remember that Rosalind was a delicately-nurtured duke's daughter. The first fine careless rapture of her love-making is perhaps a little too careless. (*Per contra:* had sixteenth century duke's daughters the Mayfair polish? Was Queen Bess herself the pink of refinement?) But what of that, so long as she hypnotises me? What of that, so long as she realizes for me, as no other actress can, the sex in Rosalind, the femineity, the *odor di femmina?* What of that, so long as she realizes for me, as no other actress can, the humour of Rosalind, the bubbling, effervescing, frolic and fun? From the first act to the last, it was the humour of the part that was brought into evidence as it had never been brought before (except, if all accounts are to be trusted, by Mrs. Jordan—another "bouncing Rosalind"). Other Rosalinds in our own time have been more tender, others more delicately refined, but surely none so humorous? The coquetry of "He calls us back again" ("He," Orlando, turning his back and certainly not calling):

the sudden gleam of fun in dropping from the "swashing and martial" to the word *outside:* the slyness of the "Who hath done this? *Is it a man?*"—a hundred such touches as these characterize Ada Rehan's Rosalind. We shall be told it is not so good as her Katherine. Truly, for she *is* Katherine : Shakespeare foresaw her advent when he wrote the part. That he did not have her in his mind's eye when he conceived Rosalind is so much the worse for Shakespeare. And if you want further answer to the objection, I return to my first one ; she hypnotised me.

"THE TAMING OF THE SHREW."

(Globe Theatre, November, 1889.)

OPPORTUNITIES of seeing *The Taming of the Shrew* on the stage are rare enough nowadays. When they do occur I make a point of doing what the late Walter Bagehot used to do when invited to one of old Crabb Robinson's literary, but not very succulent, breakfasts—I fortify myself beforehand. I mix a little less water than usual with my "Château-Poison" at dinner, and I allow myself a *chasse* after my coffee, for I know that, like Dick Swiveller's Marchioness, I shall have to make-believe very much. Man is mortal. The historic spirit is all very well, and a certain share of it is, I admit, an indispensable part of the critic's equipment. But, with the best will in the world, it is no easy task to project one's self into the age of Elizabeth, and the chattel-slave theory of conjugal relationship underlying the whole of this most Elizabethan of Elizabethan plays is a trifle too big a pill for me to swallow.

That is not the worst of it. It is my misfortune that between Shakespeare's death and my own birth (two epoch-marking dates of which the almanack-makers—*servum pecus*—have as yet only noted one) Scribe and Sardou have flourished, not to mention M. Francisque Sarcey. These ingenious gentlemen have filled my head with all sorts of notions about "dramatic construction," the *science des planches*, the "well-made" or "well-knit" play; and these notions, somehow, won't square *The Taming of the Shrew.* Was there ever such an ill-knit piece? Cannot you imagine the mincemeat Sarcey would make of it had he to review it, as a new production, in his Monday column in the *Temps?* I am not, of course, thinking of the want of sequence between the play itself and the "Induction." That is right enough; one doesn't expect a picture to fade into its frame. What I am thinking of is, of course, the fissiparous nature of the play, the lack of all coherence between the two plots —the "Katherine" and the "Bianca" plot. When one reads in Dr. Johnson that: "Of this play the two plots are so well united that they can hardly be called two without injury to the art with which they are interwoven," one can only wonder that Johnson was allowed to die a natural death. The "Katherine" plot is the story of the wooing, wedding, and taming of a termagant by a man of stronger will than her own. The "Bianca" plot is the love-story of a lass and a lad, which begins with flirtation under the cover of Latin lessons, and ends in an elopement. Give a modern dramatist these two plots to interweave and he would doubtless begin where Shakespeare does—*i.e.*, he would make the girls sisters, and he would (for the imbroglio must be mixed up somehow) make the marriage of the flirt, whom every man wants, dependent on that of the termagant, whom no one will have at any price. Problem is to find a husband for the termagant. This is where we should ask our modern dramatist to unmask his batteries.

We should expect him to show us Bianca's suitors, Lucentio, Gremio, and Hortensio (three gentlemen a little too suggestive of the Latin grammar and nouns in "io") at their wits' end to procure a husband for Katherine. After many failures, they would at length hit upon Petruchio. We should be told why Petruchio is the very man (M. Dumas would explain it to us in a short conversation between a freethinking Duchess and a fashionable ladies' doctor), and Petruchio would be brought naturally upon the stage (M. Sardou would introduce him in a gambling scene at Monte Carlo, just after he has quarrelled with his mistress, Mdlle. Trois-Etoiles, of the Variétiés). Then, of course, there would be a great scene of recrimination between the two sisters, termagant and flirt (see Mèilhac and Halévy, *Frou-Frou;* finale to Act 3), and Katherine's homily on the duties of a wife would be transferred from her own lips to those of the fashionable ladies' doctor, the *raisonneur* of the piece. Unfortunately, Shakespeare was born too soon to think of these little devices, and he makes no attempt to interweave the two plots. He simply lays them alongside one another. Lucentio, and the other nouns in "io," make no attempt to find the fourth noun of the same declension, Petruchio. He simply drops from the clouds, or, what is the same thing, from Verona. He needs no pressing from Lucentio, &c. Without any apparent motive he lays siege to Katherine, and the trick is done. The whole thing is Pre-Raphaelite in its artlessness. Perhaps the best evidence of the infelicity of Johnson's criticism lies in the fact that, on the stage, these two plots, according to him so artfully interwoven, have, until quite recently, never been presented in company. For many years the only acting version of the play was the arrangement of the "Katherine" plot, called *Katherine and Petruchio*, which Garrick made for Woodward and Kitty Clive in 1754.

Still no clumsiness of construction can prevent *The Taming of the Shrew* from titillating the sensitive palate, even if one confines one's attention to its plot. For the "Bianca" motive, with its lovers masquerading as tutors and musicians, has piquant suggestions of Beaumarchais and Rossini, of Almaviva and Bartholo, while Bianca herself is no bad prototype of Rosina. Elsewhere in the play you get what Lamb would have called a sub-indication of *L'Etourdi* and the other "Scapin" farces. This train of thought will carry you back to Plautus and Terence, while the business of the untasted meats (on Petruchio's homecoming) sends you off on another track to Sancho Panza and the Island of Barataria. In this way, while sitting quietly in your place at the Globe, you can play the truant through the literary ages.

But I have too long played truant, and have left myself very little space to talk about the doings of Mr. Benson and his company. I fear, in Thackeray's phrase, they are "rather small doin's." The company, from highest to lowest, have evidently taken great pains—they mean exceedingly well—let us give them every credit for that. But the result is, none the less, unsatisfactory. The resultant impression one gets from the performance is one of crudeness, harshness, want of harmony. Whose fault is it? Shakespeare's, partly, no doubt; but the players do not thereby stand acquitted. Mr. Benson's Petruchio is a bawling, overbearing bully. So, he may say, is Shakespeare's. But Petruchio is *playing* the bully, he is showing us how a man of spirit can get the better of a woman of spirit, he is a gentleman posing as a virtuoso in shrew-taming. All the while he should tip us the wink; he should seem to be saying, "Observe my virtuosity—isn't it good fun?—didn't I

take that note well?—mark, I beg you, the humour of
the thing." Now, Mr. Benson's Petruchio is entirely
serious: he displays no humour for us to mark.

(Lyceum Theatre, July, 1890.)

The Daly company give us *The Taming of the
Shrew*, with that "induction" which has been
practically dropped by English players since the old
Sadlers Wells days, when Phelps was seen as Christopher Sly. As Mr. Augustin Daly has not scrupled
to "rearrange" the rest of the play, it is not obvious why he has retained this superfluous introductory portion, which can only be found diverting by
the rapidly-dwindling class of fetish worshippers who
regard every word, every comma, every ink-blot from
Shakespeare's pen as inspired. But let that pass. The
representation of the play itself is an extremely vigorous, feeble: easy, laborious: finished, crude: eye-opening, soporific: magnificent and petty (here supply
pairs of contradictory epithets *ad lib.*) performance.
The first epithet of each pair is to be applied, if you
please, to Miss Ada Rehan and Mr. John Drew, the
second to the rest of the cast. The temptation to
become dithyrambic about Miss Rehan's Katherine
must be resisted. One may have the will, but scarcely
the vocabulary. One might exhaust all the resources
of the English language (and many others, both living
and dead) in singing a pæan over it. But it is better,
like the æsthete in presence of a Botticelli, to be
dumb. This mood is quite appropriate to the situation, for Miss Rehan's Katherine finds dictionary
English quite insufficient for her self-expression; she
has to resort to inarticulate animal cries, curious shrieks
in *crescendo* and (I trust I am not ungallant) grunts in
diminuendo. And there I find in her the touch of genius.

She sees that Katherine is a magnificent animal, and she has the splendid audacity to " be'ave as sich." Animalism, indeed, is rampant throughout the play. It is the great dramatic glorification of brute force. And that is why (let me, in spite of the fetish worshippers aforesaid, make a clean breast of it) the *Taming of the Shrew* gets on my nerves. There is too much brutality, too riotous animal spirits, too much jarring cacophony (whip-cracking, shouting, what-ho !-ing, and squeaking) in it for the supersensitive temperament of the fag-end-of-the-century playgoer. The scene of Petruchio, first flourishing his whip among the trembling cooks and stuttering tailors (suggestive of the popular piece of pyrotechny known as the "devil among the tailors"), and then starving his wife into submission, simply prompts me to start up in my stall, like M. Jules Lemaître in the torture-scene of *La Tosca*, and cry, " Pas cela ! C'est lâche ! " But all this, of course, is not the fault of the Daly company: it is mine. Or, perhaps (oh, sacrilegious thought !), it is Shakespeare's. Why need he have made his shrew-taming business so *criard?* Why not have relieved its asperity, its exacerbation of feeling, by an underplot of perfect sweetness and suavity, instead of giving us a Bianca *motif* which is sometimes unsympathetic, sometimes childishly complicated, sometimes simply null ? Unfortunately, these questions come too late by three centuries. Everything that can be done is done by Mr. John Drew to soften and humanize the character of Petruchio (spelled with pitiful pedantry by Mr. Daly " Petrucio "—as though to show he knows Italian better than Shakespeare. To be consistent he should have rechristened Katherine " Catarina "). Mr. Drew knows that such a part can only be made palatable by an air of obvious insincerity. A sincere, earnest Petruchio would only be acceptable to an audience of savages who have not yet passed out of the stage of marriage-by-capture.

The rest of the cast have excellent intentions, but various causes (their own physical peculiarities, the American temperament, the Declaration of Independence, and a hundred other things undreamt of in the philosophy of Stratford-on-Avon) prevent them from interpreting Shakespeare as English people think Shakespeare should be interpreted. They try to set Shakespeare to the tune of "Yankee Doodle"!—a plucky adventure, but one foredoomed to failure.

"ANTONY AND CLEOPATRA."

Princess's Theatre, November, 1890.)

THE most obvious mode of imparting an air of freshness to the criticism of a familiar classic is to run counter to orthodox opinion. Now orthodoxy, when Shakespeare is in question, means the two Samuels—Johnson and Coleridge. Of *Antony and Cleopatra* the one says that its " power of delighting is derived principally from the frequent changes of the scene," and that Cleopatra's " feminine arts " are " too low." The other, on the contrary (for it would seem that in the two Samuels—as " in the two Hinkseys " of Matthew Arnold—" nothing is the same "), finds the point of the play not in variety, but in its sustained force. " There are few of his historical plays in which Shakespeare impresses the notion of strength so much." I have, then, only to contradict these two judgments, in order to appear daringly original. I have only to write : first, the delight of *Antony and Cleopatra* is marred by its frequent change of scene, and Cleopatra's feminine arts are not low enough ; secondly, the play fails to create an impression of strength.

Unfortunately, even had I the courage to advance these opinions, they would come too late. The first of them has been anticipated at the Porte St. Martin ; the second at the Princess's. On the one hand we find

M. Sardou reducing Shakespeare's changes of scene to a minimum, and Mdme. Sarah Bernhardt lowering Cleopatra's feminine arts to the level of a Theodora. On the other we have Mrs. Langtry and her playfellows in Oxford Street persuading themselves, and conspiring to persuade us, that the dominant impression of *Antony and Cleopatra* is not an impression of strength, but one of weakness, eked out by noise and polychromatic pageantry.

As to the pageantry, let no one rashly object to it. When stage-managers hold the gorgeous East in fee, they do wisely to insist that it shall be as gorgeous as the Western purveyors of the tiring-room can make it. A generation that has been educated on Delacroix, Gautier, Gérôme, Constant, the poet of the " Orientales," and Messrs. Liberty's shop window, would be satisfied with no less. Tel-el-Kebir was not stormed for nothing. Indeed, the stage history of *Antony and Cleopatra* has always been a history of scenic display. Even the parsimonious Garrick, Genest records, went to the expense of new dresses and decorations when he mounted the play for Mrs. Yates and himself in 1759. Of the next revival (for Mrs. Fawcit and Young at Covent Garden in 1813), the chief feature was a grand funeral procession at the close, while the battle of Actium was fought in sight of the audience. So it was sixty years later at Drury Lane, when much, too, was made of processions and ballets of Amazons in honour of the nuptials of Antony and Octavia. At the Princess's the holder of the kaleidoscope is, an' it please you, an Honourable, a gentleman who is understood in what Cleopatra would call his salad days to have figured on the burlesque boards before he became Master of Theatrical Ceremonies. He thus furnishes a crowning proof of the continuity of history—inasmuch as he 'surprises by himself" two traditions of respectable antiquity, the tradition of the Roi Soleil and that of the aristocratic Choregus at the Dionysiac festivals. This gentleman, convinced, no doubt, that any sea-fight, at Actium or elsewhere, could only be an anti-climax after the Armada galleons at Drury Lane, has wisely left the battle where Shakespeare pitched it, behind the scenes.

In its stead he gives us no less than three great pictorial effects. The first is the arrival of Cleopatra in her barge, which, instead of being, as the poet designed, merely described by Enobarbus, is now (on the principle known in Green Rooms as "realizing the poster") subjected *oculis fidelibus*. Then we have the defeated Antony consoled by the glories of an "Alexandrian Festival," wherein an "Interlude, representing the conflict between Day and Night," has obviously been introduced for the express purpose of confirming Professor Max Müller's theory that our old friend the allegory on (or near) the banks of the Nile was only another sun-myth.

The third shake of the stage-manager's kaleidoscope shows the "triumphant reception" of Antony by Cleopatra after his victory. To suggest that the bearers of Cleopatra's palanquin betray an unmilitary lack of ambulance practice, or that the supernumeraries should not carry their bucklers at night precisely as they carry their advertisement boards by day, would perhaps be carping criticism. But what one must complain of is that the stage-manager, in subordinating the poem to the spectacle, has had only half the courage of his opinions. He should have wielded the scissors as freely as the kaleidoscope. A performance that lasts four hours and a quarter lasts a good hour too long. It is not a question here of reverence for

the text. Whole "lengths" from North's Plutarch
have been thrown into this play pell-mell (for there
was no thought of pleasing M. Sarcey and the well-
made-piece-at-any-price party when *Antony and Cleopatra* was written), and might with advantage be
thrown out again. For instance, some of the "alarms
and excursions" should be dispensed with, and if
Pompey, who is already restricted to one "carpenter-
scene," were banished altogether, he never would be
missed. All archaisms, too (and this play bristles with
them), should be ruthlessly excised. For all the
Princess's audience can understand of such lines as—

"By the discandying of this pelleted storm,"

they might as well be at the Italian Opera.

Mention of the opera suggests the melody of the
play. For, of course, *Antony and Cleopatra* has its
melodic scheme, just as much as Gluck's *Orfeo;* and
your Shakespearean actor, a sage has said, must
learn to *whistle* the master's verse before he can hope
to speak it. Mr. Arthur Stirling, a veteran actor
trained in the old elocutionary school, knows this, and
accordingly (due allowance made for the exaggerations
of that old school) renders the *bravura* passages as-
signed to Enobarbus with pleasing orotundity. The
"whistling" theory does not suffice Mr. Coghlan, who
shouts all his lines *fff,* forgetting that Antony's desire
to "outroar the horned herd upon the hill of Basan"
has reference only to the "savage cause" of one brief
scene. And in the very whirlwind of his passion, Mr.
Coghlan begets a temperance in a way not recommended by Hamlet. Remembering the nursery precept, that an angry disputant should count twenty-six
before opening his mouth, he is perpetually counting
twenty-six between his sentences. The abolition of

these strange pauses would probably shorten the performance by three-quarters of an hour. Mrs. Langtry's Cleopatra is not to be described as a disappointment, for the judicious can have found nothing in the lady's previous career to warrant the expectation that she could play the part. Being the Mrs. Langtry that we know, she of course realizes one-half of Dio's famous description. She is Cleopatra περικαλλεστάτη γυναικῶν, but λαμπρά τε ἀκουσθῆναι she cannot, with her thin, inflexible voice, pretend to be. Nor will her plummet-line suffice for the vasty deeps of one of the great Shakespearean heroines. She is best in her scenes of coquetry, but even that suggests the modern coquetry of Mayfair. One could not help wishing that Mr. Wingfield had retained the Queen's invitation to Charmian: "Let us to billiards;" for here was evidently a Cleopatra who had gone the round of the best country houses, and was doubtless an adept with the cue. Having written this, I light upon Hazlitt's criticism of the Cleopatra of his own day : " Her manner bordered too much on the affected levity of a modern fine lady, and wanted the passion and dignity of the enamoured and haughty sovereign." Wherefore it seems by no means impossible that the fault just found with Mrs. Langtry has been, and will continue to be, brought against every other actress in the part; the conclusion in that case being that " the enamoured and haughty sovereign " is not playable by mortal woman.

HENRIK IBSEN.

His Life.

THE controversy about Ibsen has long since become tiresome. Merely to utter his name in a mixed company is as seismic in its effects as to whistle "Croppies Lie Down" at Donnybrook Fair. Why do the heathen so furiously rage over this respectable elderly Scandinavian who lives at Munich, taking "from time to time a few whiffs at a very short pipe," in calm contempt of their raging? Why cannot they make up their minds to like him or lump him—and there an end? Meanwhile, the unobtrusive student, quietly pursuing the virtuous mean of Aristotle, would like to know something of the man about whom all the pother is being made, and he is at last in the way of having his curiosity gratified. The man's work has been carefully done into English, English of the best, by Mr. William Archer; and the man's life, in the authoritative version of Henrik Jæger, translated for English readers by Miss Clara Bell.

Jæger's book is a true biography, treating events not as isolated phenomena, but as formative influences, showing us not only what Ibsen is, but why he is. It has, of course, the defect of that scientific quality. The determination to bring even the most trivial circumstance into a logical "concatenation accordingly" is bound occasionally to result in the hunting of snarks. Thus the attempt to trace Ibsen's Puritanism to the fact that his grandfather married "the daughter of a naturalized Scotchman" is, surely, more than a little fantastic? One is reminded of the strain of " Abyssinian blood " in the veins of Dumas' Mrs. Clarkson, and chuckles. And, being a biographer, Jæger is apt to take his subject too seriously. When Ibsen was a youth (and an apothecary's apprentice), his soul was like a star and dwelt apart, as the souls of clever apprentices have a trick of doing. "At a ball," we read, "while his companions gave themselves up to pleasure and enjoyment, he would stand meditating on all the sorrow and misfortune which lurked in the background beneath the cheerful surface, wondering how many of the dancers were waltzing only to forget their woes." "Happy villagers!" sang the gloomy Stranger in the old burlesque of Kotzebue's play—

" Happy villagers, dance away!
Fits may follow—
But dance away!"

One would give something for a sketch of Ibsen at the Ball, by Mr. du Maurier. On the whole, however, Jæger is sane enough; he sees his subject steadily, and sees it whole. The one drawback (for English readers) is that he sees it at somewhat too close quarters. Being himself a Scandinavian, Ibsen's environment, Ibsen's temperament, Ibsen's *ethos*, are familiar to him. To us aliens these things are unfamiliar, and we want them explained from our point of view. If only Jæger's grandfather had married the daughter of a naturalized Englishman!

Certainly Mr. Podsnap would have swept all Ibsen's characters behind him as un-English. They are all, men and women alike, so deeply concerned about the condition of their own "dirty little souls," all introspective, all wondering why they came into the world, and what is their mission in life, all touched with a certain austere melancholy. I own myself quite unable to imagine Nora Helmer buying Christmas cards at the Stores, or Consul Bernick on the knifeboard of a Brixton omnibus. Are Norwegian people, I wonder, really built that way, and if so, why? For the melancholy, Ibsen's childish surroundings are no doubt partly accountable. He was born in the market-place of Skien, with the school on one side and the church in the centre; "to the right of the church," he writes himself, "stood the town pillory, and to the left the town hall, with the prison and the lock-up for mad persons." The only amusement of the boys of Skien, apparently, was to steal water-logged boats—evidently a place far behind Peebles for " pleesure and deevilment." Some not very profound persons have expressed surprise that the new dramatic gospel should have issued from so remote a Nazareth. Surely, if a new drama was to come, it is precisely from such a quarter, away from the main current of European life, and far from the madding crowd who drink *bocks* outside the Café Américain, that one would have expected to get it.

Always excepting the Latin countries, the dramas of Ibsen have overrun the Continent of Europe to the same triumphant extent as have Wagner's operas. According to a Norwegian journalist, Mr. Harald Hansen, no less than a dozen treatises have already been written on Ibsen's theatre: one in Norwegian, one in Danish, two in Swedish, five in German, one in Polish, one in Dutch, one in Finnish—without counting innumerable articles in every language. The significance of this is not to be missed. The success of Ibsen's theatre means the dethronement of Paris from the position of theatrical supremacy which it has held undisputed for two centuries and a half. *Delenda* —if not *deleta*—*est Theatropolis!* Racial antipathy is at the bottom of this, I suppose. The secret discontent of the blameless Hyperborean with Latin life as reflected in Latin dramatic art, has now burst into open revolt; he has at last got a dramatist of his own. And one seems to hear him shouting to the played-out Caucasian of the boulevards, " Whaur's your Sandy Dumas the noo?" Or yelling, with the crowd of Ramanticists at the Français on the night of February 11, 1829, "*Enfoncé, Racine!*"

The blameless one hails Ibsen as destined to play Luther to the Leo X. of Dumas *fils*. As we all know, the great Frenchman poses as moralist even more than as artist, and Ibsen challenges him on both counts. They both deal with the great sexual question; but what infinitely greater sincerity and scope there is in the treatment of it by the new man! He shows us relations between modern men and women far more interesting than the one relation of animal appetite. For him the *Ewig Weibliche* is concerned with far more complex matters than the Seventh Commandment, divorce, and the affiliation articles of the Civil Code. To the author of *L'Ami des Femmes* and *L'Homme-Femme*, who takes the Oriental view that woman has no soul (or, " Please, sir, a very little one "), and, plagiarizing from the curate Edward Bull, thinks her sole duty is to be the bondwoman of man, Ibsen retorts with *A Doll's House*, demonstrating her right to be herself. And whereas the Frenchman and his fellows can never get the *odor di femmina* out of their theatre, Ibsen will turn his back on the women for awhile, and, in a *League of Youth*, a *Pillars of Society*, an *Enemy of Society,* diagnose social diseases in which they have no concern. (Here, however, the average sensual man, not so blameless as the Hyperborean, whispers that he would welcome Ibsen's muse more warmly if she were a trifle more voluptuous. The women of the new dramatic dispensation are flat-chested, and have a little too much of "that damned intellect.")

It is on the side of theatrical craftsmanship that one might have expected the Frenchman to have the advantage, heir as he is to all the traditions of the first stage in Europe. Yet here, again, he is beaten. Throughout the Fifties, first at Bergen and afterwards at Christiania, Ibsen was a stage-manager. He rehearsed over a hundred plays, and so acquired, no doubt, his astonishing *technique*. As Jæger truly says, his plays (*i.e.*, his social dramas, the only ones here in question—for Ibsen the poet, the Ibsen of *Brand*, of *Peer Gynt*, of *Emperor and Galilean*, I have not the effrontery to tackle) begin where ordinary plays usually end; they are all in fact "amplified catastrophes." What an immense gain this is to their Unity of Impression (the sole modern representative of the classic Three) needs no demonstration. As for his dialogue, we get on his stage the talk of real life —at last! The little fishes do not talk like big whales, there are no epigrams, there is no *raisonneur*—a De Jalin, a Rémonin, a Des Ryons—introduced for the express purpose of letting off conversational fireworks about *vibrions* or *pêches à quinze sous* ("Yet," sighs our average sensual man, returning from Paris by the Club train, "I cannot help a sneaking affection for that old *raisonneur* of Dumas—unless, like Thouvenin, he becomes a *raseur*"). Just one more comparison. In the art of subtle, ironical presentation of character there is not a Frenchman who can touch Ibsen.

Augier, perhaps, came near him, once, in *Maître Guérin*. But what is one such portrait to a gallery-full of Stensgaards, Bernicks, Helmers, Gregers Werles? True, the irony is sometimes too subtle for the weaker brethren, as the bewildered demeanour of many of the audience on the first night in London of *A Doll's House* testified. Indeed, some critics, I understand, are still convinced that Torvald Helmer was hero and martyr. Let Dr. Ibsen put that in his "very short pipe" and smoke it!

"ROSMERSHOLM."

(Vaudeville Theatre, February, 1891.)

IBSEN, in the circles of English Podsnappery, is waved aside as a Chimæra, but those of us who are still prepared to erect altars to any sort of unknown god (automatic, of course, in the underground stations — with a slot for the worshipper's penny), think of him rather as a nineteenth-century Sphinx. He has the fascination of the inscrutable, the mysterious, the enigmatic. Now the Sphinx is quite a new Idol of the Theatre. The average modern play, on the psychological side—when it has any psychology at all, which is not often—is as plain as a pikestaff; its moods, its emotions, its currents of thought, are carefully focussed to the vision of *l'homme sensuel moyen*, the ten-pound householder, the gentleman who always takes an unfair share of the room on the knifeboard of the omnibus. Ibsen, on the other hand, empties out on the stage a bag of entirely new psychological tricks; with him new-fangled philosophies, religious aspirations, hitherto only dimly perceived by the Englishman in books (mostly "on grey paper with blunt type"), are for the first time seen in the playhouse; obstinate questionings of invisible things are for the first time heard there. And, along with his new subject-matter, he has brought a new *technique*. It is because, then, of the novelty of his theatre, because he is a "strong man," an athlete, lifting heavy philosophical weights where such weights have never been lifted before, and because he lifts them in calm contempt of all the old orthodox laws of theatrical gymnastics, that so many of us are attracted to Ibsen; not, as a vain people supposeth, because we approve the conduct of his personages, or regard ourselves as the addressees of his ethical "message"—whatever that queer missive may be. We take a purely æsthetic delight in him, because he gives us new impressions. There is an impressionist in one of Mr. Henry James's novels, whose *animula vagula blandula* is summed up in this way : "I drift, I float, my feelings direct me—if such a life as mine may be said to have a direction. Where there's anything to feel I try to be there!" Well, dramatic criticism just now is impressionist; it is drifting and floating. There is always something to feel in the playhouse, when Ibsen is being played, and we try to be there.

The novelty of Ibsen's method must have leapt to the eyes of those who visited the Vaudeville Theatre when *Rosmersholm* (translated by Mr. Charles Archer) was played for the first time on the English stage. Baldly and brutally stated, the story is by no means new. An adventuress, Rebecca West (not Sharp), establishes her footing in Rosmersholm, a household where the Rosmers, husband and wife, suffer from what the Divorce Court records call incompatibility of temper. By innuendo and suggestion Rebecca succeeds in convincing the wife that she is *de trop*, and that the best thing she can do is to efface herself and so leave her husband free to wed his kindred soul, the adventuress. Brought to this conviction, Mrs. Rosmer throws herself into the mill-race at the end

of the garden. After living for a while in a Fool's
Paradise, Rosmer learns from external sources that
his wife has committed suicide not, as he supposed, in
a fit of madness, but in order to make way for Rebecca.
That lady's own confession then opens his eyes as to
the share she had in the tragedy. Of course, there is
only one end to all this. Poetic justice must be done.
To expiate their crime, hers of deliberate intention,
his of blind folly, they both follow the dead woman
into the mill-race.

How this theme would be treated on our native
stage it is not difficult to guess. We "drive at
practice," as Jeremy Collier was the first to say, and
the material, mechanical side of the tragedy would be
the side for the English playwright. The scene of
"the Bridge by Moonlight" (with real water) would
be the *clou* of the piece. The adventuress (as Mr.
Jerome K. Jerome knows) would wear sky-blue satin,
smoke cigarettes, with her feet on the table, and probably push Mrs. Rosmer into the mill-race *propriâ
manu*, as Lady Audley pushed the gentleman down
the well. She herself would be drowned in the mill-
race by accident (what time she came down that way
to gloat over the late Mrs. R.), and Rosmer would be
drowned in trying to rescue her. Then an old family
servant (or the "comic man," reformed) would come
in with a Bible, and say, "The wages of sin is death."
Curtain.

In Paris, they would try another way. There
would be no "stupendous mechanical effects." Everything would be done by talk, and within four walls,
as everything is actually done in Ibsen's play. But
the personages would not talk much about themselves;
they would exchange repartees and listen to a long-
haired poet reciting *décadent* or *déliquescent* verses,

while they themselves would be explained and commented on by a third person, a sort of lecturer without the wand. But both French and English playwrights, be sure, would have one thing in common: they would both begin at the beginning, *i.e.*, start with Rebecca's entry into Rosmersholm, and show us Mrs. Rosmer in the flesh.

Now turn to Ibsen, and see how fresh, how audacious, his treatment is. He starts—where the undergraduate's Ibis walked safest—in the middle, and works backwards. Mrs. Rosmer's suicide has occurred some time before the curtain rises, and for a good half of the play "the enigma of the mill-race," as one of the personages calls it, remains unsolved. Through two entire acts we are left without any hint that Rebecca is not what she seems, that she is other than a "sympathetic" character. It is not until the third act is nearly over that we discover that it was this apparently harmless young lady, with the mild demeanour and the advanced Liberal opinions, who practically sent Mrs. Rosmer headlong into the mill-race. And why she did it we do not learn until just before the curtain finally falls. Note that, whatever we learn, we learn at first hand, from the characters themselves, not from a Dumasian commentator or *raisonneur*. Ibsen's personages always explain themselves, analyze themselves, put themselves under the microscope, pull themselves up by the roots to watch how they are growing, eviscerate themselves to see where the golden eggs come from. They are for ever asking themselves: Why did I come into the world, and what (to speak as M. Paul Bourget doth) is my *état d'âme?* And what a curious, remote "soul-state" that is! When we come to examine it, we find that the plot of *Rosmersholm* which I, purposely, began by stating in terms of vulgar melodrama, serves Ibsen as the sub-structure for nothing either vulgar or melodramatic, but for a veritable Soul's Tragedy. Rebecca is found to have established herself in the Rosmersholm household because, if you please, she saw there scope for the development of her "views," because Rosmer would make her a useful intellectual companion—what academic youth calls a "reading-chum." "I wanted to take my share in the life of the new era that was dawning, with all its new ideas. We two, I thought, should march onward in freedom, side by side. But between you and freedom rose that dismal, insurmountable barrier——," Mrs. Rosmer. Hence the tragedy of the mill-race. Note, too, that the old concept of free-will, which had found a last place of refuge in the theatre, is now finally abolished, Rebecca has a metaphysical explanation for her conduct, pat. "You think I was cool and calculating and self-possessed all the time! I was not then the same woman as I am now, as I stand here relating it all. *And then there are two sorts of will in us, I believe!* I wanted Beata away; but all the same I never believed that it would come to pass. And yet I *could* not stop. I *had* to venture the least little bit further.—*That is the way such things come about.*" One cannot listen to that sort of thing without recognizing in Ibsen a new stage-force. All his drama is internal, the evolution of successive "soul-states." Even Rebecca's confession is not brought about, as in other hands it assuredly would be, by external means. She simply makes it to restore to Rosmer (whom she has learnt to love) his sense of "innocence," to lift from his mind the consciousness of guilt which prevents him from continuing his life-work of "ennobling human souls, making every man in the land a nobleman." Of course she is not troubled by any feeling so old-fashioned and unscientific as mere remorse. There can be no remorse where there has been no free-will. Rosmer, too, has his own soul's tragedy in his conversion, under Rebecca's guidance, from conservatism to liberalism, from orthodoxy (he is a retired clergyman) to freethought. All this is very piquant, *bizarre*, fresh, of absorbing interest to the serious spectator, and to the more eclectic *dilettante* (say the Des Essarts of M. Huysmans), at least as fascinating as a Japanese curio or the rare edition (uncut) of the " Pastissier Françoys." One feels that Ibsen's people are ourselves, yet not ourselves. They are intensely human, yet intensely Scandinavian—much farther from us English, with their introspection, their gravity, their melancholy, their morbid intellectuality, than the mere extent of the voyage by steamer from Hull to Bergen. No wonder the blither spirits among them, the Ulric Brendels and the Ejlert Lövborgs, take to drink, for they breathe an atmosphere, in Johnson's phrase, of "inspissated gloom."

"HEDDA GABLER."

(*Vaudeville Theatre, April*, 1891.)

THE latest of Ibsen's social dramas differs in formula from the earlier members of the series. The most novel and noteworthy feature, from the technical point of view, of such plays as *The Pillars of Society*, *A Doll's House*, *Ghosts*, and *The Wild Duck*, was the author's peculiar use of the ironic method in the exposition of character. In one play Ibsen takes a model citizen, Consul Bernick; in another a model husband, Torvald Helmer; in a third, a model exponent of conventional morality, Pastor Manders; in a fourth, a model enthusiast for truth-at-any-price, Gregers Werle — and, when first introducing these characters on the scene, he takes care that we shall not suspect them to be anything other than models. Then—sometimes gradually, sometimes abruptly—he opens our eyes to the real weakness, vice, or even criminality, which these models of conventional virtue, when put to certain tests, exhibit. This method, involving as it does a temporary deception of the audience, sins against one of the oldest canons of orthodox dramatics (see, *e.g.*, Diderot's preface to the *Père de Famille*, and Lessing's remarks in his *Hamburg Dramaturgy*, on "theatrical surprise-strokes"). But as a weapon of ethical warfare there can be no question of its deadly efficacy.

The shock to the audience, upon the sudden exposure of the seamy side of its pet moral ideals, is tremendous. There is nothing of this in *Hedda Gabler*. Of the character of its eponymous heroine we are never for a moment in doubt. Even before her first appearance on the scene we are led to suspect, and immediately after it we are clearly shown, that she is what the old stage-jargon called an "unsympathetic personage." Her "face and figure," so runs the stage direction, are "dignified and distinguished." But the "colour of the skin is uniformly pallid." Then her eyes are "steel-grey, with a cold, open expression of serenity." And her hair, though "of an agreeable brown," is "not very thick." The wary playgoer is at once prepared to find that the cold serene eye means hard ferocious egoism, and that the thin hair leads to violent jealousy of a certain Mrs. Elvsted, whose hair is "unusually copious and wavy." So when Hedda describes Mrs. Elvsted, as "She with the irritating hair, which she went about and made a sensation with," we are not surprised at the malicious outburst, though we may be at Mr. Gosse's English. There are, however, less flimsy reasons than those of capillary repulsion for Hedda's dislike of Mrs. Elvsted. The latter is, to use Hedda's (or Mr. Gosse's) expression, an "old flame" of Hedda's husband, George Tesman. She is also a new flame of Ejlert Lövborg, George's most dangerous rival in a competition for a coveted professorship, while Ejlert, in his turn, is an old flame of Hedda herself. It seems that Hedda has married George—a harmless, rather fatuous bookworm—merely in the hope of escaping from *tædium vitæ*. "The only vocation I have in the world," she says, "is to bore the life out of myself." The exercise of feminine jealousy comes as a welcome relief from boredom.

Thea, *alias* Mrs. Elvsted, the lady with the irritatingly "copious and wavy" hair, has inspired Lövborg to write a book, which is understood to be an epoch-making work, though at present it is only in MS. Hedda, whose jealousy is exasperated to frenzy by Lövborg's description of this MS. as "the child—my child and Thea's," practically steals it, after inducing Lövborg to return to the old dissipated courses from which Thea had rescued him. She then throws it, sheet by sheet, into the fire, whispering—"Now I am burning your child, Thea!—you, with your curly hair!" And when Lövborg enters, distracted, not only by the loss of his work, but by the sudden ruin (through a drunken brawl with the police) of his professional prospects, Hedda hands him a revolver, telling him to shoot himself—"and do it beautifully." The story of Hedda's jealousy occupies three acts of the play; the fourth, and last, brings the inevitable penalty. Lövborg is dead; "the child" is burned. But Hedda is not stricken with remorse. Ibsen is too great an artist for that; he shows us how the whole mischief worked by the woman is simply the necessary outcome of her own nature. ("You see, it takes me all of a sudden," she somewhere says, "and then I *can't* help doing it.") To Hedda's mind, the real catastrophe is that the mischief leaves her no better off than before. Rather the worse. Mrs. Elvsted has kept the notes of Lövborg's MS., and, with George's help, is going to reconstitute the work, as a monument to the dead man's memory. And Hedda finds that the boredom of her old life is likely to become degradation; for a certain Judge Brack, discovering that the pistol found on Lövborg's body is Hedda's, uses his knowledge as a threat to force her into a shameful intimacy. But she has another pistol left, and, putting it to her temple, she ends her miserable life.

The "hard-shell" Ibsenites, who insist upon regarding Ibsen as a moralist rather than as a dramatist, will be sore put to it to find the moral of *Hedda Gabler*. More wary persons, who recognize that the purpose of art is not to point morals, but to create impressions, will be content to accept the play as a picture of a peculiar type of *révoltée*, a dramatic study in mental pathology, a nineteenth-century tragedy. A *Quarterly* reviewer prefers to consider it an exhibition of "realism in its most extravagant and possibly its most shameless form." Such epithets as "shameless" and "extravagant" are part of the stock vocabulary of the old judicial school of criticism; but they have absolutely no meaning to those of us who think that literary criticism is not some dominie-business of assigning good and bad marks, but the art of enjoying masterpieces. *Hedda Gabler* is a masterpiece of piquant subtlety, delicate observation, and tragic intensity, and I take leave to enjoy it. Its heroine may be, as our judicial critic asserts, "a monstrous specimen of unfettered womanhood;" but I can only ask "What then—so long as she is interesting?" She is a very complex, very modern, very morbid type; and if you ask me whether she is to be praised or blamed, I put aside your question as a pure irrelevance—she is to be watched with interest. Here is a woman who, out of the mere desire to escape from the boredom of Philistine surroundings—a Scandinavian Eustacia Vye all forlorn upon an Egdon Heath of moral monotony—wrecks another woman's happiness, drives a man to disgrace and death, and finally puts a bullet in her own brain. All this, because she had thought to import some colour and excitement into a world all too wan and dull by "moulding a human destiny." There is the type—to take or to leave. Ibsen has simply drawn it to interest you, not to point any moral whatsoever. The play is a bit of sheer "impressionism."

"THE LADY FROM THE SEA."

(Terry's Theatre, May, 1891.)

IBSEN'S *Lady from the Sea* is understood to have been the result of a holiday visit to the sea-side. It is a respectable trophy to have brought back from a bourn whence most travellers return with nothing more noteworthy than a few bloodthirsty specimens of the familiar fauna of a Margate lodging-house. But it is not, for all that, a convincing play. One does, perhaps, detect a whiff of ocean in it, but no more than a whiff. The experiment of "sea water at your own doors" seems to be as hopeless an enterprise in literature as it is, I believe, in commerce. Ellida Wangel, the mermaid-heroine of the play, who finds the waters of the fiord "sickly," and declares (in curiously Bostonian English) that she "belongs out there," *i.e.*, to the vasty deep, should be, metaphorically, dripping with brine, or, in Hedda Gabler's figure, have seaweed in her hair. That was doubtless the author's intention. Two obstacles, however, seem to have prevented its successful realization, so far as it is to be divined from Mrs. Eleanor Marx Aveling's version of the play. One is the lack of an actress of genius sufficient to make a plausible mermaid. "When you've once for all become a land-animal, it isn't so easy to find your way back again to the sea," as the mermaid says; and actresses are necessarily land-animals. The other is the incongruity between this mystic Venus Anadyomene and her prosaic nineteenth-century surroundings. Ibsen the poet, the Ibsen of *Brand* and *Peer Gynt* we know, and Ibsen the sociologist we know ; here he has attempted to "double" the two parts, with only half-success. Poetry and sociology will not, it seems, amalgamate. Taken as a fragment of sociology, the play suggests an alternative catastrophe to *A Doll's House*. Had Torvald Helmer, instead of expostulating when Nora threatened to leave him, politely replied, "Go by all means, my dear," opened the front door for her, and offered to assist her into the Scandinavian equivalent for a hansom, it is possible that she would have elected to stay at home. That is practically the procedure of the husband towards a wife of vagabond temper in many familiar pieces—in *Brutus, lâche César*, in *Divorçons*, in *La Petite Marquise;* but these are frivolous plays, and Ibsen (one must make his adversaries a present of this damaging admission) is nothing if not serious. Accordingly, the lady's roaming disposition is promoted to the dignity of a "craving for the vast and infinite," an "awakening and growing need for freedom." These are the fine phrases of her husband, who bids her choose "in freedom and on her own responsibility" between himself and the embodiment of "the vast and infinite"—a burly American sailor in knee-boots, who has exercised a mysterious facination over the mermaid since, years before, he plighted his troth with her by flinging his ring, together with hers, into the sea. Thus presented with her freedom, the wife, mystic mermaid though she is, behaves precisely like the frivolous ladies in the Palais-Royal plays I have mentioned. "Freedom ! Responsibility !" she says, "that transforms everything!" and, straightway casting off the American sailor and all the nostalgia of the sea which he had represented for her, she falls into her husband's arms, determined henceforth to be a land-animal and a good little mother to her grown-up step-daughters. As a contribution to the great Husband and Wife Question, the moral of the play will probably be claimed by both parties. It has the double charm of the famous impressionist picture in *La Cigale* (of Meilhac and Halévy, not Audran) which, according to the end you turned up, represented either red sunset over a blue sea or the tawny desert under an azure sky. Wives with a velleity for emancipation will say that the play concedes the right of elopement. The husbands, unspeakable Turks to a man, will retort that the concession of the right destroys the sole motive for its exercise.

In any case, people with a keen scent for irony will be able to find what is ostensibly a serious sociological drama "full," like Jeames de la Pluche's conversation, "of lacy ally and easy plesntry." Two minor figures are genuinely comic. A boyish sculptor coolly asks a damsel to remain single, and "to think of him" sympathetically, during his 'prentice years. "It would help me so much, as an artist," he explains, "the knowledge that somewhere in the world a young, exquisite, silent woman is secretly dreaming of me; and she, having no special vocation in life, can so easily do it." Ultimate marriage with the exquisite and silent woman is no part of his scheme. "When I've made my way, she will be a bit too old for me, I fancy." Therefore, when she has duly encouraged his artistic development, she is to stand aside, that he may marry her younger sister. A characteristic touch of grim humour is added to this by the fact that the sculptor is, all unaware, dying of rapid consumption. Equally diverting in another way is the younger sister in question, who finds the sculptor's ignorance of his impending fate, the anticipation of wearing mourning for him, the bald spot on her tutor's head, and, indeed, every gruesome or trivial feature in the Cosmos, "fascinating." Compared with these subalterns, the major personages of the play are failures. The mermaid-wife and her Yankee merman are embodied dreams; and dreams (except when a Shakespeare dreams them o' Midsummer Nights) fade in the garish light of the stage. The husband I am prompted by the unspeakable Turk within me to call a poor hen-pecked creature. The tutor with the "fascinating" bald spot is a bore. No final judgment, however, can be pronounced on the play until it has been properly played. With every desire to recognize the excellent intentions of the players at Terry's, one is unable to accept their performance as anything like an adequate representation of *The Lady from the Sea.* They are all too obstrusively—land-animals.

ALEXANDER THE GREATEST.

ARE we ever going to have sober-balanced views about the elder Alexandre Dumas? Shall we ever see that Colossus steadily and see it whole? Time was when any stick was good enough to beat Dumas withal: the loaded cane of "Eugène de Mirecourt," the bludgeon of Granier de Cassagnac, the dominie's birch of M. Ferdinand Brunetière, and even the twopenny switch of Mr. Percy Fitzgerald. For these and their like he was a Minotaur of other men's virgin reputations, the Father of all Lies, the masculine of the Scarlet Woman, and at best a sort of inspired "nigger-minstrel." Then came the inevitable reaction, and behold Dumas transfigured, the deformed transformed, by Mr. W. H. Pollock, Mr. R. L. Stevenson, Mr. W. E. Henley, and others, into a godhead, a nineteenth-century trinity of which the first person is Panurge, and the second Pantagruel, and the third Brother John of the Funnels! In pouring their libations on the altar of this new Dionysus—(for a pagan simile will perhaps be more seemly)—ordinarily grave frock-coated essayists become appropriately dithyrambic. It needs only Mr. Swinburne with his full-mouthed superlatives to complete the orgy. These excesses on either side send the average sensual man distraught. They pervert his usual pursuit of the Ibis (walking safest in the middle) into a wild-goose chase. They tempt him to herd with vestrymen or to read "In Darkest England." He will do better to read Dumas' account of himself. That way, and only that way, safety lies. If he have French enough, let him read it in the original ten volumes of "Mes Mémoires" (Paris: Lévy). If not, Mr. A. F. Davidson's abridged translation in two volumes (London: W. H. Allen) comes pat to the occasion. This is a selection from the first five volumes of the original, ranging from the year 1792, when Dumas' father was appointed General-in-Command of the Army of the Western Pyrenees, to 1829, when his father's son produced *Henri III. et sa cour* at the Théâtre Français. It is, perhaps, just as well to warn the reader whose acquaintance with Dumas is yet to make (happy man!) against undue expectation. He will find in Dumas' memoirs little, if any, introspective analysis. The autobiography of the prince of egoists, strange to say, does not belong to the literature of egoism. Dumas was not a self-revealer, like Montaigne, or Pepys, or Rousseau. Neither was he a self-tormentor, like Stendhal, Macready, Amiel, Marie Bashkirtseff. He has not bequeathed his laundress's bills to future generations, like the Barras of his own delightful anecdote, nor his dinner *menus* and doctor's prescriptions, like the Messieurs de Goncourt. As he said of himself, he is *tout en dehors;* he presents you only with the outside of the platter. But he does not go through the Pharisaic exercise of washing it beforehand. He does not spare himself. It is his friends whom he spares. The result is a history for the most part in dialogue or *oratio recta*, where occasionally the speaker, no doubt, is made like the "passon" to say "whot 'a owt to 'a said." The translator artfully pleads Thucydidean precedent. I should rather detect, what some one else has detected in Sardou, *la doigtée du dramaturge*—the fingering of the playwright. But history, of a sort, it is: first, of Alexandre Dumas himself; and, second, of the great Romantic movement.

Theories of the evolution of the Romantic movement are, in the poulterer's phrase, "cheap to-day." They can be had while you wait: are given away with a pound of tea. Some of course are more ingeniously wrong than others. Only make your definitions of "classical spirit" and "romantic spirit" wide enough—calling them, for instance, with Mr. Pater, "the quality of order in beauty" and "the addition of strangeness to beauty"—and you can find the origin of the Romantic drama in Sophocles, or, for all I know, in the Primeval Chaos. Or, at least, you may carry it back to Rousseau's "Confessions" with M. Brunetière, or, with M. Deschanel, to the tragedies of Voltaire. Or again, taking Sydney Smith's "short views," you may be content to start with Mdme. de Staël's "De l'Allemagne" in 1815. I for one ask leave to choose that date partly as a good patriot, because it somehow seems to connect the Romantic movement with "the thin red line," and partly because it fits in with the particular theory of the movement that best elucidates these memoirs of Dumas. The theory in question—I encountered it last in the sober pages of the late M. J.-J. Weiss—is, briefly, that the Romantic movement was the result of the "driving in" of the fever of Napoleonic adventure. When Napoleon's impulse towards the East—his *Drang nach Oesten*—was finally arrested in 1815, the French spirit turned from Romance in action to Romance in imagination. In other words, the French went through a course just the reverse of

Mr. Squeers's pupils—they first cleaned w-i-n-d-e-r, winder, and then went and spelled it. Bonaparte became Buridan. Mind, it is not I who am responsible for this engaging theory. I only adopt it here because it exactly covers the ground of Mr. Davidson's two volumes, and because it brings into the Romantic movement not only Dumas the elder, who was there before, but, for the first time, Dumas the eldest. I am not sure that I ought not to write Dumas the greatest. (If I did I should at least have the companionship of the gentle Anatole France.) We have had enough and to spare of comparisons between the elder and the younger Dumas (Mr. Pollock's Alexander the Great and Alexander the Coppersmith, and the like), but of the grandfather, the first Alexandre, even veteran Dumasqueteers betray the most shameful ignorance. This man was an ideal soldier of the Republic. Twenty months after he had enlisted as a private he was a general. At the age of thirty he was a commander-in-chief. He captured the St. Bernard by assault. He held the bridge at Clausen single-handed against a whole Austrian regiment, and so was dubbed the Horatius Cocles of the Tyrol. When he led his troops up Mont Cenis, "every man had rolled on his knapsack a shirt and cotton cap. This was my father's uniform when he went chamois-hunting at night. Arrived at the palisades, the soldiers began to clamber up; but my father, thanks to his Herculean strength, found a simpler and less noisy plan, which was to take each man by the seat of his trousers and by his shirt-collar and to throw him over the stockade." Tartarinesque, of course, and Gahagantic; but, laugh as you will, the man was a hero. He quelled a revolt at Cairo by riding his horse into a mosque at a hand-gallop, earned the dislike of Napoleon by his stern republicanism, and was poisoned in a Neapolitan prison. In short, he cleaned the w-i-n-d-e-r which his son was to spell. Then this weary Titan came home to Villers-Cotterets, and three years after the birth of "our dear Dumas" died neglected and in poverty. To descend from such a man is to be predestined to greatness. What is best in Alexander II and Alexander III you will find in Alexander I.

The second of the dynasty is shown in Mr. Davidson's volumes as he was when Villers-Cotterets did his green unknowing youth engage; they leave him at the moment when Paris claimed him in his riper age. Not a chapter of his country life could be spared. Napoleon changed horses at Villers-Cotterets on the way to and from Waterloo: on purpose, it would almost seem, that young Dumas might record us a wonderful "impression" of the great man. In his sporting adventures the boy out-Winkled Mr. Winkle. His first tavern-bill at Paris was paid with the game he shot on the road. There is a story about a pair of breeches even droller than that about the postilion's which Mr. Brooke recommended to Dorothea. Of Dumas' early attempts at play-writing, when he came to Paris as a copying-clerk in the establishment of Duc d'Orléans, it ought to be superfluous to speak. The *Mémoires* leave one with the feeling that for the literary aspirant this was the Golden Age. It all reads like an Arabian Night's Entertainment. You knocked off a vaudeville between your sips of absinthe at the *café* opposite the Français. Then you would mortgage the author's rights in advance to old Porcher, whom you would find in another *café*. Or you might capture Baron Taylor in his bedroom, and read him your five-act tragedy while he sat helpless in his bath. If you strolled into a theatre to see a play of Charles Nodier's you might, with ordinary luck, sit next to an old gentleman who, when not buried in the Elzevir *Pastissier Françoys* (which long haunted the dreams of Mr. Andrew Lang), would hiss the piece, get turned out for his pains, and prove to be no other than Charles Nodier himself. The literary aspirant might be discouraged or encouraged; but he was never ignored. The mugwump of letters had not then been invented; everybody had to take sides. The King's brother did not disdain to be on yours, nor His Majesty himself to be against you. Surely, never since the days of the Antonines had principalities and powers been so literary? Napoleon's "pit of Kings" at Erfurt, 'tis clear, had not been forgotten. On the first night of *Henri III. et sa cour* the Duc d'Orléans retained the whole of the circle, and stood up, bareheaded, to hear the author's name announced. Dumas' own account of this *première* reads so like a fairy tale as to have been long suspect. But the testimony of eye-witnesses (*e.g.*, Alphonse Royer and, quite recently, Charles Séchan) have since confirmed it in every particular. The boxes fetched twenty louis a-piece. The Malibran could only find a place in the third tier: she was seen leaning right out of her seat, and, to keep herself from falling, holding on to a column with both hands. Victor Hugo and Alfred de Vigny had not been able to get seats; Dumas found room for them in his sister's box. All these glorious visions and more you may enjoy in *Mes Mémoires*.

DUMAS FILS.

HOW to qualify him ? A dramatist who can give Scribe and Sardou points and a beating at their own game ; a prophet who has brought down new Tables of the Law from a Sinai hard by Mont Valérien ; an apostle whose prefaces, pamphlets, articles, are so many Epistles to the Lutetians; moralist, philosopher, mystic, dabbler in occultism, deist, socialist, conservative—to be thus prodigal of differences is to be a mere centre of perplexity, a rallying point of the bewilderments. To Montesquieu's Persian or Goldsmith's Chinaman his whole theatre would seem one prolonged nightmare, and his pistol-practice a criminal waste of good powder : they would untie the knot of his dramas by tying a knot in a bow-string—or by adding a new wing to the harem. But with the passage from Ispahan to Paris, from polygamy to monogamy, the great conflict of sex passes from a mellay to a duel : a code of honour, seconds, a doctor, and occasionally the police, come upon the ground. Dumas *fils* is always the doctor, sometimes the police, very often the judge. Of course it is the weaker combatant that absorbs his interests— the Eternal Feminine, to wit. He prescribes for her, and when she rejects the drug he throws the Code and the Bible at her head, calls her the Beast of the Apocalypse, the female of Cain, and other hard names —" wich is plenty, Dudley James." He began, as the

May of youth and the bloom of lustihood will, by putting his head in the Beast's mouth—to show how easily she could be tamed. The result of his experiment was *La Dame aux Camélias*. To the play-going Fifties this seemed, of all things in the world, a realistic play: they took it for a new approximation to the truth. So thinks every generation of its own drama; Sophocles was a realist in the eyes of a people bred on Æschylus. But *la Dame* is not the beginning of Realism as we know it, rather is it an end—one among many—of Romanticism. Marguerite is a true daughter of Marion Delorme; and, as you know, she died childless. The play, by its author's admission, is dead; and *Le Demi-monde*, masterpiece as it was, is only half-alive. The social half-world it depicts is merged in the general mob; its famous *pêches à quinze sous* are mingled pell-mell with the other contents of the fruiterer's stall; the very name has changed its meaning—for the worse. In its time it showed the whips of the elder Duval turned to scorpions in the hands of Olivier de Jalin. But Suzanne d'Ange seems now a more pathetic figure than Marguerite; and Olivier de Jalin—in M. Dumas' eyes 'le plus honnête homme que je connaisse'—has long been voted an egregious cad.

The revolt of the polygamous (or the polyandrous) instinct against the official monogamy of the West: the revolt, its pardon or its punishment—that is the true subject of the living Dumas and his theatre. It is of course the subject of many other dramatists; but in his unswerving devotion, his postponement of every ology to the pathology of love, he is the master of them all. To examine his theatre is an exercise in permutations and combinations. You have so many fixed elements: husband, husband's mistress, wife,

wife's lover; you combine these elements in all possible ways, and to each way corresponds a play of Dumas *fils*. The first group of combinations gives the woman taken in adultery. Here that Bible M. Dumas is so fond of quoting would teach him not to throw stones; but that Bible of his does not include the New Testament. He must have blood. At first it was the lover's: in *Diane de Lys* Paul Aubry falls the first victim to his pistol-practice, Diane herself being let off with a fainting fit. Then came the lady's turn: Diane was spared because a something of the old romance still clung about her; she was of the family of the Indianas and Lélias—a lamb not ready for the shambles. But in the Iza of *l'Affaire Clémenceau* (written by M. Dumas in book form, but subsequently dramatised by M. Armand d'Artois) and in the eponymous heroine of *La Femme de Claude* the lamb became the Beast, and Clémenceau's jade-handled dagger, Claude's new patent breechloader, did their work, and the gospel of *tue-la* was preached unto the nations. Then emerged (not perhaps in strict chronological sequence: the mental development of this *homme ondoyant et divers* contemns the almanac) a new theory of the Adulterous Woman: she was to be saved from herself by her superior, Man. This theory, long held by M. Dumas and much misunderstood when first promulgated in *l'Ami des Femmes*, is not new. It is a theory which gives Dumas a point of contact, after all, with our friends the Persian and the Chinaman: it is the harem theory, or rather its Western counterpart, the "Doll's House" theory flouted by Ibsen. Dumas' statement of it is that man is "le moyen de Dieu," woman only "le moyen de l'homme." Of herself she has no soul: man alone can help her to get one. Her business is to obey, his to command.

Illa sub, ille super. Hence, when started, as so inferior and naturally perverse an animal cannot choose but start, on the high road to adultery, she must not be allowed to reach her destination and so get stabbed like Iza or shot like Claude's wife : she must be pulled up short by a sympathetic, omniscient, omnipotent male friend, who talks like a (boulevard) angel. Jane de Simerose must be saved by M. des Ryons, and restored by stratagem to her husband's arms. Or this weak animal, woman, " qui ne sait pas," is to be saved by her sympathetic male friend, " l'homme qui sait," through the latter's Josephic self-denial until what time the husband (who is a brute) shall be conveniently suppressed. That is the strange situation of wife, lover, and husband in *l'Etrangère*.

With the peccant husband the theorist of *l'Etrangère* has a short way. An American *deus ex machinâ* (one of Febvre's best works) kills him " like a little rabbit." Two acts out of three plainly foreshadow the same end for the husband in *La Princesse Georges ;* but here M. Dumas at the last moment shirked his own logical conclusion : M. de Terremonde's pistol-shot brings down not the wicked husband but a harmless, unnecessary " walking gentleman." Then came a great change. The Oriental theory of woman's inferiority was suddenly abandoned for another (also Oriental), " an eye for an eye and a tooth for a tooth." This is the actual text quoted by the betrayed wife in *Francillon.* The peccant husband shall not be slain— either personally or vicariously : his wife shall claim the same liberty to break the Seventh Commandment as himself. Here again, however, the nothing-if-not-logical Dumas fights shy of his Q.E.D. The wife, put to the touch, does not enforce her claim : she only shows that she could an if she would : they kiss again with tears; and the husband, no doubt, goes on *da capo*. One study of adultery M. Dumas has in which there is no question of pardon or punishment: the *Visite de Noces*, a remarkable exposition in one act of the real reason why the husband of a virtuous woman is tempted to " go Fanti." It stinks in the nostrils of the Philistine; but the fumes of the acid will not blind the judicious to the amazing vigour of the etching.

With a new set of elements, M. Dumas puts down his Bible for his Code. That authority forbids, or forbade, "la recherche de la paternité"; so M. Dumas falls to discussing the moral obligation of a father to acknowledge his illegitimate offspring. The hero of the *Fils naturel* demands paternal recognition and is refused; rising to fame, he is offered the recognition, and refuses it in his turn. In *Monsieur Alphonse* what the actual father refuses the mother's husband grants in his own name. In close connection herewith is the question of the *fille-mère*. She is the heroine of two of M. Dumas' most interesting plays, *Les Idées de Madame Aubray* and *Denise*, in both of which it is the unexpected—the marriage of Dorothy Musgrave not to George Austin but to John Fenwick —which happens. And with such skill does his father's son " prepare " his climax that there is not a man nor a woman in the audience who does not ardently desire this marriage to be made.

For—to turn from Dumas the moralist to Dumas the artist—this man's mark of primacy in stage-work is that he has the supreme gift of interesting. No more than his father does he ever shirk the *scène-à-faire*, he invariably " prepares " his situations, he takes you safely over the weak places with a rush, he forces you to accept the most impossible conclusions in spite of your severe senses. It is useless for you to object : the protest you are grumbling to yourself in your stall he puts into the mouth of one of his characters—the fool's for choice—and, lo ! you are answered. His style—hard, brilliant, plangent, admirably minted and chased—is the very style for the garish day of the footlights. Its one defect is a tendency to lapse into the jargon of pseudo-science, as when he discourses of "le vibrion." Science, indeed, has always been his weak point. He believes in table-rapping and chiromancy. You see, he never had a university training, and is perhaps a little too proud of it. M. Bigot thinks he got his science from the *feuilleton* of the *Figaro*. But the plain truth is he is a born dramatist, and knows that the "shy" sciences are dramatically effective from their very mystery. As for wit, he is as prodigal of that as his father was of that and money. He lavishes it on all his personages, even on the very lackeys. Sheridan did the same, and you love him none the less for it. In the invention of "bravura" passages, meant to catch the ear of the town, Dumas has no equal : the "pêches à quinze sous" of the *Demi-monde*, the theory of "la ligne" in *Madame Aubray*, the "chasse à l'ours" of the *Danicheff* are cases in point. Unlike his father, he works best alone. Who shall say whether he will or will not live ? For forty years he has dramatised us every strategic movement, every decisive engagement, all the alarums and excursions, in the great war of Love against Law. The strife will doubtless last "our time," and his fame along with it. For in truth he has practised his art with an abounding sincerity. That is, he has done his best to be great.

SARDOU.

WHEN La Bruyère said that "the making of books is as much a trade as the making of clocks," he obviously plumed himself on having achieved a startling paradox. But he reckoned without the rival aphorist who said that paradox is only commonplace in the making; and—naturally, for it is no part of your philosopher's business to foresee the inevitable — he reckoned without Sardou. With Sardou play-making is not merely as much a trade as clock-making; it is the same trade. Sardou has perfected (the doubtful honour of its invention belongs, of course, to Scribe) the clock-work play. Perfected, because Sardou is a master of the trade to which Scribe was only an apprentice: he speaks with authority and not as the Scribes. But authority just now (now in this connection being a smug euphemism for all our yesterdays and to-morrows) is hardly a word to conjure with, and Sardou's is certainly on the wane. Young France will have none of him. He has been found guilty of the well-made piece, and there are many previous convictions against him. Another reason for his crucifixion is that he is an Impenitent Thief. Not only has he perpetrated well-made plays, but he has stolen his ideas, as the boy stole the brooms, ready-made. He cannot even plead benefit of clergy, for he has not M. Zola's "literary esteem."

Of his thieving there is overwhelming evidence.

The record is as glorious reading as the "Newgate Calendar." Did he not crib the idea of the *Pattes de Mouche* from a story of Edgar Poe's? And *Les Pommes du Voisin* from a novel of Charles de Bernard's? And *Séraphine* from one tale of Diderot's? And *Fernande* from another? Is not *l'Hôtel Godelot* a French, a very French, *She Stoops to Conquer?* He may even, Harpagon-wise, apprehend himself on suspicion of self-robbery. For did he not appropriate a situation in *Séraphine* from his own *Vieux Garçons?* And steal the first act of *l'Oncle Sam* from the first act of *La Famille Benoîton?* His impenitence, too, is not less flagrant that his crime. In his letter to M. Jouvin (preface to—suggestive title!—*Les Pommes du Voisin*) he raises impenitence to the dignity of a theory : the theory of originality in plagiarism. "The right of the dramatist to seek inspiration in subjects previously treated in other literary forms is consecrated by immemorial usage ; the process of transforming a story into a dramatic action constitutes a creation, a new paternity. Dramatic art consists less in the choice of subject—necessarily restricted to seven or eight primordial situations, which have gone on repeating themselves ever since Adam—than in the original development which rejuvenates them ; from Hamlet, who is Orestes, to old Goriot, who is King Lear, there are not two works which can be said to have sprung fully armed from their author's head, owing nothing to any one." But this suggested comparison of himself with Æschylus, Shakespeare, and Balzac is, of course, only M. Sardou's modesty. The best answer about his plagiarisms he has made vicariously, through the mouth of M. Sarcey, who points out that borrowing is no such easy matter since you or I don't do it. What! There were plays to be stolen from this, that, and the other quarter—plays which could run hundreds of nights. We knew this all the time and yet allowed M. Sardou to bag and make millions by them! What idots we are!

Sardou has not only a theory for his thieving and a theory for his impenitence: he has a theory for his well-made piece. A play, he says in his preface to *La Haine*, "invariably appears to me as a sort of philosophic equation from which the unknown quantity is to be disengaged. This problem possesses me, and lets me have no peace until I have found the formula. The formula once found, the piece follows of its own accord." This sort of jargon is always expected from a French dramatist when he writes a preface; but an artist in clock-work should be the last man to seek noon at fourteen o'clock. Read: Given the tension of the main-spring and the dimensions of the wheels, and the clock follows of its own accord. Here, however, M. Sardou is really too modest. The clock does not follow of its own accord: the clock may come but it won't *go*, unless the formula has been found by the right person; and the right person is the *homme de théâtre*. Who is the *homme de théâtre*? M. Zola defines him as "a man who conceives subjects in a particular fashion, outside the truth; a man who dances on the ends of needles, who wins a bet that he will make his personages walk on their heads; a man whose trade it is to falsify everything he touches; a man who runs counter to the real tendency of literature and degrades himself to curry favour with the crowd." But then M. Zola does not love M. Sardou overmuch; he has never been even so much as suspected of the well-made piece. No, the *homme de théâtre* is the man with the fingering of the playwright, the man with the scenic instinct, the man who has studied theatrical projectiles and their ranges, so that he can tell to a hair's-breadth how far they will carry over the footlights. And M. Sardou is pre-eminently that man.

When it is he who finds the formula, you may depend upon the clock going, and for considerably more than eight days. There are formulas and formulas, but Sardou's is practically one. He starts with two acts of exposition : acts of gay, even brilliant, comedy, which fix the framework and social environment of the piece. Expect in these two acts to be diverted by the humours of a bustling multitude ; for M. Sardou has something of the Napoleonic faculty for manœuvring crowds. Then come two or three acts of drama. A little late, you think, this appearance of the action only when the play is half over. But you must blame the dinner-hour, not M. Sardou. People are never in time, he says, for the rise of the curtain, and he does not care to develop his intrigue until all his audience are seated. Here is another instance of the early bird catching the worm. For M. Sardou's first act is generally superior to the rest ; his frame to his picture ; his types to his intrigue. Contrast the first act of *Maison Neuve* or of *Fernande* with the rest ; the framework of *La Famille Benoîton* or of *Odette* or of *Georgette* with the picture ; the types of *Nos Intimes* or of *Nos bons Villageois* or of *Les Bourgeois de Pont d'Arcy* or of *Thermidor* with the intrigue : and oblige M. Sardou by dining earlier in future. Note in these first acts, or first two, of framework M. Sardou's fancy for superficial satire and for the "actuality" of the moment. As a satirist he is superficial because it is not the fundamental, eternal vices of human nature which he attacks. These he leaves to a Molière or an Augier, confining himself to contemporary crazes : particularly to the Second

Empire craze for luxury and social swagger, as in *La Famille Benoîton* and *Maison Neuve*. His fondness for actuality has earned him the nickname of the "barometer playwright." Mr. Brander Matthews and other ingenious persons have pointed out the connection between the political reaction of 1872 and that admirable and delightful *Rabagas*; between the foreign spy mania of 1877 and *Dora*; between the Macmahonite wire-pulling of 1878 and the *Bourgeois de Pont d'Arcy*; between M. Naquet's Divorce Bill of 1881 and *Divorçons*. The prohibition of *Thermidor* shows, perhaps, that in 1891 for once he failed to read the barometer aright.

M. Sardou's enormous output during his thirty odd years of playmaking comprises comedies, opera "books," *féeries*, historical dramas, political satires, eighteenth-century *pastiches*, thesis-plays, innumerable five-act dramas of modern life, and, in these latter years, a whole series of violent melodramas fitted to the measure of a particular actress. His rate of production, always rapid, perhaps touched its maximum in the Sixties. In 1860, for instance, he brought out *Monsieur Garat* at the Théâtre Déjazet in April, *Les Pattes de Mouche* at the Gymnase in May, and *Les Femmes Fortes* at the Vaudeville in December. Again, in 1865, he produced five acts in January (*Les Vieux Garçons*, at the Gymnase) and five acts more in November (*La Famille Benoîton*, at the Vaudeville). Out of all this how much will survive? Little, perhaps, beyond the memory of Sardou's one really great invention, tne dramatic paper-chase. His tricks with love-letters are brilliant feats of sleight-of-hand. Think of the great letter trick in *Fernande*, in *Les Vieux Garçons*, in the last act of *Dora*. Above all, think of that wonderful Odyssey of the *billet-doux* in

Les Pattes de Mouche. It is hidden under a statuette, which serves the lovers for a letter-box. Who will be the first to snatch it? the woman who wants to get it back or the man who wants to use it as a weapon? The man it is ; but he is induced by the woman to light his cigar with it. Thrown half-burnt out of the window, it is picked up by a naturalist and converted into a prison for a beetle. Another lover purloins it to write a second message on its blank side. And finally it passes into the hands of the woman's husband, who reads the wrong side of it, while you ejaculate " Saved ! saved ! " This is the sort of thing which will immortalise Sardou. It constitutes his one indefeasible claim to be considered a man of letters.

"LA TOSCA."

(Lyceum Theatre, July, 1889.)

IS the portrayal of physical torture artistic? To this question, which is one that every performance of *La Tosca* inevitably provokes, the answer seems to be : it all depends upon the medium employed. The Laocoon portrays physical torture, and the Laocoon is art. " Salammbô " portrays physical torture, and "Salammbô" is art. The pre-Raphaelite pictures of grilled, disembowelled, and arrow-riddled saints in the National Gallery portray physical torture, and these are art. Why, then, do I feel that the representation of Cavaradossi's torture by the minions of Baron Scarpia in the third act of *La Tosca* oversteps the limits of art, and becomes mere bestiality, a mere appeal to the lust for blood which lurks low down in all of us as the last proof of our kindred with a Nero and a Caligula? Is it not because here the medium becomes one of absolute realism, because the dramatic is a closer approximation than any other art to the crudity of actual life ? I leave Mr. Grant Allen and the other professors of physiological æsthetics to settle the question ; I can only record the fact that the yells and screams of Cavaradossi, with his head encased in the " Luke's iron crown " of Baron Scarpia's inquisitors, revolt me just as the groans of a man run over by an omnibus in Cheapside revolt me, just as the sight of the blood gushing from a disembowelled horse in the Plaza de Toros at Valencia once revolted me. No; inhuman butchery on the stage is not art —or, at least, is no art for me; with the sickening smell of the shambles in my nostrils I can give no thought to merely æsthetic emotion. And that is why, despite all the constructive dexterity of Sardou, despite all the perfervid intensity of Sarah Bernhardt, I not only do not like the third act of *La Tosca*, but absolutely loathe it, and am glad to escape into the (comparatively) fresh air of the Strand, where the 'bus conductors' cry of " Penny all the way " assures me that the great mundane movement is going on without a suspicion (unless it be to the horses on Ludgate Hill) of torture.

Once more, is the exhibition of physical agony within the proper province of dramatic art? Some years ago, when Mrs. Rousby was burnt at the stake as Joan of Arc in Tom Taylor's play, the same question was raised, and again it was heard after the treadmill scene in Charles Reade's dramatization of his own " Never too Late to Mend." The answer each of us will give seems, at first sight, to depend upon two things. The first thing is, our susceptibility to the illusion of the stage. If we have none of that, *cadit quæstio*. We are not to be affected by pain which we know all the time to be a sham. And the less we have of that so much the less are we affected. The second thing is our degree of sympathy for physical suffering in real life, and this, I think, will be found really to include the first. For lack of sympathy for another's pain means lack of imagination, lack of power to put yourself in another's place —a lack which, whether it arises from an iron nerve or from mere thickness of skull, is likely to blunt your susceptibility to stage illusion. Mind, I do not suggest for a moment that the converse holds good. A low degree of susceptibility to stage illusion need not imply imperfect sympathy with real suffering, for in some cases, of course, it will proceed not from mental sluggishness, but from over-familiarity with the inside of the playhouse.

The two opposite attitudes which the bulk of mankind take up in the presence of the cruel infliction of physical pain are well illustrated in a passage of that fascinating little book, "The Story of an African Farm." The boy Waldo is stripped, tied up, and viciously thrashed by his tyrannical master. "Tant' Sannie" (the unimaginative Boer woman) "felt half sorry for the lad ; but she could not help laughing, it was always so funny when any one was going to have a whipping." The highly-sensitive little girl, Lyndall, quivers with sympathy and revolt. "She kissed Waldo's naked shoulder with her soft little mouth. It was all the comfort her young soul could give him." Tant' Sannie would have watched the torture-scene in *La Tosca* unmoved ; Lyndall would have sickened and turned from it. Lyndall, in the present case, is M. Jules Lemaître, of the *Débats*. What Lemaître says is practically this: that the stage presentation of extreme physical suffering is outside the domain of art for the simple reason that the feeling of repulsion it excites in the spectator is so strong, so all-absorbing, as to leave no room, at the moment, for any other emotion whatever. There are only two ways of controverting this. Either it may be said that horror, *per se*, is an artistic impression, which is nonsense; if the word "artistic" is to have any meaning, or it may be denied that the horror is felt. The latter position is the one taken up by Mr. William Archer, who, though anything but a Tant' Sannie himself, has gratified a passing fancy for paradox by becoming the spokesman of the Tant' Sannie class. Let me take his chief points in order.

(1) It is playfully suggested that we who profess to dislike the torture-scene in *La Tosca* are more or less unconscious humbugs. We are like the butcher in Dr. Johnson's saying, "Sir, a butcher will tell you that his heart bleeds for his country, when, in fact, he experiences no inconvenience." (Johnson was a typical Tant' Sannie. His robust and cross-grained temperament had no sympathy with real physical suffering, and made him notoriously impervious to the illusion of the stage. There is no need for me to cite anecdotes from Boswell to prove what every one will admit.) There is, of course, no refuting the charge of insincerity or self-deception. A says he is horrified; B says A is either romancing or deceiving himself. B's only ground for the statement is apparently the fact that he himself is not horrified, which is no argument.

It is hinted (2) that our feeling of repulsion, granting that it exists, ought to be conquered by our admiration for the playwright's marvellous intellectual adroitness, for the perfection of his stage mechanism. Certainly *La Tosca*, as a whole, is a clever, a diabolically clever, bit of stagecraft. But we are not discussing the play as a whole, we are discussing one particular scene, and in that scene I can see no particular stagecraft whatever. Given the situation —Mario being tortured on one side of a door, the Tosca beating helplessly against it on the other as she listens to his cries—the dramatist has absolutely nothing to do. There can be no dialogue, for the situation is too strong for speech. No one hears the few words the Tosca utters, for she is reduced almost at once to inarticulate shrieks and sobs. She tears her hair, drags herself along the floor, writhes in frenzy, or stands stock-still in mute despair—a fine bit of pantomime for the actress, if you like, but no opportunity for the playwright's "intellectual adroitness." As Lemaître says, any one might have written this scene—anyhow.

Again (3) the torture-scene ought not to distress us, because "the one thing we are sure of all the time is that there is no real suffering in the case at all. We know that Mr. So-and-so is not being tortured behind the scenes." Quite so, and that knowledge prevents us from doing what, without it, we should do at once, namely, bounding on the stage, handing the actor who plays Scarpia over to the police, and sending his victim off to Charing Cross Hospital on a stretcher. Nobody is so silly as to petend that either in this play or in any other is there actual delusion. But there is illusion, and illusion sufficiently strong to give us much of the sensation we should experience in presence of the real thing itself. Whatever may be said about poetic tragedy (which is not here in question), there is no gainsaying that the be-all-and-end-all of realistic drama is illusion. And if *La Tosca* be not a realistic drama, what is it? For my part, I found the realism of the torture-scene so perfect that it was with the greatest difficulty (believe it or not who may) I persuaded myself that Mario was *not* being tortured behind the scenes. I had to reason with myself something in this way: "You idiot! Why are you so distressed? You know very well that there is no Mario Cavaradossi lying outside there, strapped to a couch, with his head in an iron circlet. It is really Mr. So-and-so, a young actor at so many pounds a week, who is probably, at this moment, taking a steady pull at a tankard of stout, or perhaps glancing over the evening paper." And yet I could not shake off the overmastering horror of the scene.

Finally (4), the torture business ought to leave the spectator unmoved, because Sardou has not induced him " to regard Mario Cavaradossi and Floria Tosca with that intimate affection which makes their sufferings, as it were, personal to him." As if, in a case of the infliction of atrocious physical suffering, it mattered twopence to the onlookers whether the sufferer is a sympathetic person or not! Even if it were the monster Scarpia himself who was being tortured, my loathing of the scene would remain unchanged. For what is the feeling at the bottom of one's instinctive repugnance to witnessing the torturing of one man by others, whether in real life or in the imitation of the stage? Is it not the feeling of secret humiliation at the idea, thus vividly brought home to one, of the abject impotence of all the nobler parts of man—all those elements of mind, character, that make him a being of large discourse, looking before and after—in the presence of such a miserable accident as mere brute force? One's pride in our common humanity is outraged.

ALPHONSE DAUDET.

"LA LUTTE POUR LA VIE."

(*Her Majesty's Theatre, June,* 1890.)

NOTHING of M. Daudet's stage work, inferior as that is, both in quantity and in quality, to his output as a novelist, can safely be neglected. His plays strike some of us as good, others of us as bad, but no one can reckon them as indifferent. If only as a ringleader in the modern revolt against classical stage tradition, against the theory of the "well-made piece," against the dogmas of the *homme de théâtre*, against the *scène-à-faire* and the whole Sarceian creed, M. Daudet is enormously interesting.

First impression of *La Lutte pour la Vie*. The play will be noteworthy in that little chapter of history which will some day have to be written under the heading "Science and the Stage," or (if you like an alternative alliteration), "Darwinism and the Drama." Its mere title shows that the purveyors of the playhouse have at length heard of the theory of evolution. M. Daudet's hero, or rather, protagonist, Paul Astier, illustrates the application of what he supposes this theory to practice. The spectacle of the immorality of the blind forces of nature, of the destruction of the weak by the strong, the unfit by the fit, in the struggle for life, suggests to Paul that he should "go and do likewise." Nature has no conscience, he argues, therefore, why should I have? So he seduces one woman (under his wife's roof), goes very near to poisoning another (the wife whom he has married for her money), uses all men unscrupulously as his tools, is, in fact, a monster of selfishness, and airily fathers all his crimes on the back of Darwin. Poor simple-minded, domestic sage of Beckenham! What an affiliation! Paul even gives himself what he supposes to be a Darwinian name. He is a *strugfor-lifeur!*

It would be unfair to identify M. Daudet too closely with his stage-puppet. Yet I cannot help thinking that he, as well as Paul, has fallen into the old confusion of thought; that the double meaning of " law " has been too much for him; that he vaguely supposes that a law of science is like a law of the land, a generalisation the same thing as a precept. To be sure, he introduces a young, scientific man, Antonin, who undertakes the defence of Darwin against this monstrous parody; but it is a very bungling defence. I note, too, that Antonin stutters, wears ill-made clothes, cuts a sorry figure before men of the world, and is, in short, the conventional scientific man *à la* Dumaurier. Another little fact throws a flood of light upon M. Daudet's scientific attainments. He makes one of his personages speak of " Berkeley and the other *Scotch* metaphysicians."

This sort of thing will make "dramatist's science" as great a by-word as "dramatist's law." It is an old story. Take M. Dumas *fils*, the only predecessor of M. Daudet who has systematically brought science on the stage. "I have studied spiritualism," he once said, "as I have all the other *sciences*." He classifies chiromancy with the differential calculus. Think of Doctor Rémonin and his theory of the *vibrion* (*L'Etrangère*) : think of the lady who explains her temperament by the "Abyssinian blood in her veins" (*Princesse Georges*). And, coming nearer home, think of the wonderful toxicology to be found in Mr. Grundy's *Fool's Paradise*, or of the hundred and one forms of cerebral disease, unknown to the faculty, to be found (what time the will goes a-missing or the villain has to be identified) in any English drama you please. In this respect, then, M. Daudet is no worse than his fellows. And he is no better.

Do I, then, conclude that dramatists should leave science alone? By no means. Only, instead of adopting it as a theme, and getting fogged in its technicalities, let them bring its spirit into their method. Let them abandon the arbitrary, the uncaused, the *deus ex machinâ*, the nick-of-time miracle, and what Mr. Haddon Chambers called in *Captain Swift*, the "long arm of coincidence." Let them show the characters and actions of their personages, not as mere pawns and moves on a chessboard, but as the inevitable resultants of the interaction of organism and environment. Let them note the way in which modern science has changed and transfigured modern conceptions of morality. Is not that change mainly a substitution of law for chance, of a fixity of order in the universe of things for the old notion of free-will? The novelists have long since seen this. Hence the profound modification of the novel to be found first in George Eliot, and later in Emile Zola. And even the playwrights are, at last, becoming alive to it. They are, tentatively, beginning to show how faults are not the consequences of "original sin," but the inevitable outcome of circumstances (including, of course, previous faults); *e.g.*, Mr. Grundy in *A White Lie*, and Mr. Pinero in *The Profligate*. We may look, I think, for an early modification of the stage villain. The wicked man is, scientifically regarded, a sick man and an unfortunate man. If it were not that to mention Ibsen (the most scientific in method of all dramatists) exasperates many worthy people to frenzy, I would instance Krogstad in *A Doll's House*.

Second impression of M. Daudet's play. The novelty and complexity of its stage-"business." It simply bristles with stage directions—a distinct mark of modernity. Take up a Shakespeare or a Molière, and you shall find the fewest and simplest of stage directions. *Enter 1st Citizen. Exeunt omnes. Alarums and Excursions. Noise without. Dies.* That is about all. M. Daudet directs the pantomime of his personages as minutely as he does their dialogue. You remember the story of Diderot, who attached so much importance to pantomime that he stuffed his ears with cotton-wool the better to judge the value of a play. And the modern stage is gradually recognising this importance. Constrast *The Dead Heart* of Mr. Walter Pollock in 1889 with *The Dead Heart* of Watts Phillips in 1859; the talk has been diminished while the stage-"business" has been expanded by fifty per cent. Two of the most important scenes in *The Struggle for Life* — important because they explain and develop the character of Paul Astier— are contrived as dialogues between Paul and his secretary, the one while he is "off" (in his bedroom, whence he answers the secretary, who is bustling about the stage), and the other while he goes through the process of dressing for dinner. The latter scene is a most elaborate bit of "business." Paul enters half-dressed, warms his curling-tongs with the spirit lamp, "fixes" his moustache, gets his secretary to help him with his tie, never uttering more than monosyllables or fag-ends of sentences. But the methodic coolness with which he goes through this process, adjusting a shirt stud while he describes his mistress's attempt at suicide, gives you more of the character of the man than volumes of words. Very effective, too, is the "business" of the *dénouement*. The scene is at an auction, and the dialogue of the personages at the footlights is punctuated by the bids of the crowd in the background, while the auctioneer's "Going! Going!" is a perpetually recurring refrain. A pair of pistols is put up, and knocked down to a bidder who has entered unobserved. It is Vaillant, the father of the girl Paul has seduced. The auctioneer's sing-song of "Going! Going!" continues while the old man walks slowly down the stage. He fires, and as Paul falls stone-dead, down comes the auctioneer's hammer with a solemn "Gone!"

Third impression. That when I described M. Daudet as a rebel against classical stage traditions, I spoke too hastily. I ask myself these questions. Why, when Paul Astier tries to poison his elderly wife, the ex-Duchess Padovani, does his courage fail him at the last moment? M. Daudet says it is partly owing to his dress-coat, *i.e.*, the conventional restriction of his surroundings, partly to his age, *i.e.*, he belongs to the men in the Thirties, who have not yet cast off all the old superstitions and traditional moralities. For my part, I feel that Astier refrains from poisoning the Duchess simply because of the exigencies of M. Daudet the playwright. Had he carried his criminal intent through to the bitter end, the Duchess's fine scene of warning and pardon could not have been written. The exigencies of M. Daudet the playwright, there I think you have the key to the whole business—and note that they are as often as not the exigencies of the old-school conventional playwright. The Duchess's detection of the secreting of the bottle of poison by Astier; the device by which she induces him to attempt the crime (she feigns illness and asks him to fetch her water at the moment she knows he has the poison in his pocket); the final pistol-shot by which poetic (yes, the old, old poetic, not Darwinian) justice is executed on Paul Astier—all these things belong to conventional melodrama. M. Daudet himself is too fine a critic not to have an uneasy consciousness of this. At the reverberation of the pistol-shot, he imagines some young cynic in the audience exclaiming, "Bravo, D'Ennery!" Well, I would "go one better" than that youthful cynic, and cheerfully shout "Bravo, D'Ennery!" at many other things in the play beside the pistol-shot. Once more, why drag in Darwin? Paul Astier is a stage type who was old centuries before the doctrine of the struggle for life was invented. He is merely the unscrupulous egoist, the man who, in pursuit of his own ends, will stick at nothing, will spare no man's life, no woman's virtue. Have we not had Molière's Don Juan, Shakespeare's Richard, Feuillet's Camors, and fifty other such types. But the worst of it is that the commanding qualities that the dramatists have actually shown us in these men have, in Paul Astier's case, to be taken for granted. All the women, we are told, are dying for love of him, all the men fear him, and we are all the time puzzled to understand why. He says nothing very clever, his manners are not seductive, his dress waistcoat is abominably ill-cut, his frock coat is in the fashion of the year before last, and, to crown all, he is represented by an actor whose presence is the reverse of imposing. Surely a very feeble *homme fort!* A lathe painted to look like iron! And, once again, why drag in Darwin?

JULES LEMAÎTRE.

"MARIAGE BLANC."

(*Royalty Theatre, June*, 1891.)

YES, I suppose it is true enough, if one condescends to think of it in that way, that M. Jules Lemaître's *Mariage Blanc* is a morbid play. The epithet has been hurtling through the air of late, but it falls ludicrously wide of the mark. When are we to get rid of this old superstition that the drama is nothing if not didactic? The moralist who complains that a play is not wholesome may be quite right from his point of view. So may the logician who complains that a sonata is not a syllogism. But æsthetic criticism passes these objections by as sheer irrelevancies; at least, as *ultra vires*. It refuses to regard a work of art as anything but a work of art. It calls nothing common nor unclean. There is no room in its vocabulary for those overworked adjectives. Morbid? The *Œdipus Tyrannus* is a morbid play; so is *Hamlet;* so is *The Cenci;* so is *Une Visite de Noces*. You see, so many sides of life are morbid, and that Curious Impertinent, the artist, will insist upon looking at life from every side and touching it at all points.

And the worst of it is, that the older art grows the more "morbid" it is likely to become. By this time it has explored most of the high roads of life; it must needs turn at last into the by-paths—the nooks and corners. After the normal, the abnormal. After the loves of Edwin and Angelina, interrupted by stern parents, but set, in the last act, to the tune of marriage bells and a tag from the comic retainer, one is nothing loth to consider less cheap and obvious histories of the relations between men and women— as, for instance, M. Lemaître's history of the relations between Jacques de Thièvre and Simone Aubert.

Jacques is a descendant of that Signor Pococurante who was so hospitable to Candide. A sheer hedonist, he finds that by the age of five-and-forty he has exhausted most of the pleasurable sensations which life has to offer. Naturally he is a sceptic in the matter of woman's love. He is capable of having dictated to M. Paul Bourget some of the most cynical reflections in that elegant philosopher's treatise on *L'Amour Moderne*. When he confesses his no-creed to one of those benevolently sagacious physicians who are even more common in modern French plays than in Thackeray's novels, the usual advice is bestowed upon him. Up and be doing something useful; cultivate the simple emotions; take a wife. Had he followed this advice in the spirit in which it was given, he would have been not himself but the hero of another play, M. Gondinet's *Un Parisien*. He does take a wife, but only because the taking offers his jaded palate the prospect of a new sensation not to be looked for in any ordinary kind of matrimonial tie. He proposes marriage to a young consumptive girl who has only a few months to live. Needless to say, neither the girl's physician nor her mother approves the proposal. It seems to them freakish and—one cannot escape the word, you see—morbid. So, to be sure, it would be, and worse, if Jacques were contemplating an ordinary marriage. But (although he does not say so) he has read the latest gospel of Count Tolstoy, and hastens to explain that he only designs a spiritual union. Poor Simone Aubert, whose girlish innocence is not surpassed by that of the heroine in the familiar " I, too, have not been idle " anecdote, will never know that her marriage is not as complete as other women's. Her last moments will have been consoled with at least the illusion of love. And Jacques will have captured that Snark for which he is perpetually hunting, a new sensation, the sensation of contact— asymptotic, to speak as the geometers, rather than tangential — with a little Dresden china piece of innocence. The mother and the physician give way; not so Marthe Aubert. This young lady presents the opposite type to her sister Simone's. She is as physically strong as the other is weak, a woman of sensual temperament, passionately desirous to taste of the joy of life. In a word, she wants a husband badly, and, for choice, Jacques de Thièvre. On the disclosure of the projected marriage, her whole nature surges up in revolt. All her life she has been sacrificed to Simone, has been turned into a mere sick nurse, and has seen all the mother's affection bestowed upon the invalid. And now her sister is to rob her of the man she loves! Her protests do not prevent the marriage, such as it is, from taking place; but even then she is not to be balked. She confesses her love to Jacques, and practically throws herself in his way. A far more conscientious man than Jacques de Thièvre, one must admit, would find his virtue sorely endangered by such a trial. Charles Surface, you remember, said that, in such a juncture, he would probably have to borrow some of Joseph's morality. Jacques seeks to temporise, and puts Marthe off with a clandestine appointment for that evening. Whether he would ultimately have to borrow any of Joseph's morality or not we shall never know; for Simone overhears the appointment, and the shock kills her on the spot. So may you expel Nature with a fork, by the experiment of a spiritual marriage with a consumptive Simone, and yet will she recur in the person of a full-blooded Marthe.

Even if one did not know that M. Jules Lemaître is an expert of experts in the art and mystery of dramatic criticism, I think one might find enough of internal evidence in *Mariage Blanc* to show that it is the work of a man familiar with all previous plays, and a little tired of them all. He fastidiously avoids the beaten theatrical tracks. He will not make his physician a *raisonneur*, with a cut-and-dried pseudo-scientific theory, for that would be only to repeat M. Dumas *fils*. Literary pyrotechnics having been overdone by M. Pailleron and others, his dialogue shall be natural, pedestrian, a little brutal. M. Octave Feuillet would have converted Jacques, after marriage, from cynicism to gushing sentiment. Wherefore M. Lemaître is careful to leave him unchanged. The spectacle of Simone's innocence, the utter self-abandonment of Marthe, only draw from him a quiet little ejaculation of "Tiens! tiens!" The temptation of introducing a big dramatic *scène des deux sœurs* must be avoided; partly because M. Sarcey would insist upon the necessity for it, and partly because it would have to be a reminiscence of the third act of *Frou-Frou*. The play must show true *lemaîtrise*, be all new. Of its novel details, perhaps the most daring is the frank immodesty of Marthe. To put on the stage a young girl (not an adventuress) who unblushingly reveals her anxiety to get married, and her intimate knowledge of what marriage is (see, for instance, the scene in which Marthe "pumps" Simone for confidences about the secret relations between herself and her husband), is to give a general audience a slap in the face. Audiences, like Mrs. Chump, object to being slapped. Wherefore the epithet "morbid" continues, and will continue, to hurtle.

W. E. HENLEY AND R. L. STEVENSON.

"BEAU AUSTIN."

(Haymarket Theatre, November, 1890.)

"AT the beginning of August, 1823," writes Thackeray, "Bartlemytide holidays came, and I was to go to my parents, who were at Tunbridge Wells." Three years earlier he would have met Beau Austin there, and so learned a truer diagnosis of the dandy than the famous one of the layers of waistcoats superimposed on nothing. Austin would have pointed him the way to the dandy's heart. In their play of which the Beau is the eponymous hero Messrs. Henley and Stevenson map out that route for us, working their little chart of the dandy's *pays du tendre*, sampler-wise, in silk traceries on delicate faded stuffs. It was high time, for the dandy has suffered from a conspiracy of misinterpretation. Indeed, one might almost call him the male, not as some have lightly thought him, of the society beauty, but of the *femme incomprise*. Thackeray did him wrong, Bulwer no less, Macaulay and Carlyle of course, even George Meredith. He was never an Admirable Crichton. He was not an aristocrat, and his royalty, though real, was not of the sort catalogued in the *Almanach de Gotha*. He was more—he was a Warwick. "I have made this man what he is," said

Brummell of Alvanley's fat friend, "and I can unmake him." The elder Richmond had been a king of dandies, but he was tempted to be Richmond Roy, and lost his dandyhood. "*Roy ne puis, prince ne daigne, Brummell suis,*" was your true dandy's motto. George Austin knows this, for though he has travelled to Tunbridge in the chariot of a royal duke, that vehicle is to him only "another person's carriage," and he is held to have "brought the duke in his train." History has gone wrong over the dandy quite as grievously as the less pretentious form of fiction. The dandy disdained public affairs. Wherefore Alcibiades and Bolingbroke, with claims otherwise valid, are ruled out of the game. As *grands seigneurs* Lauzun and Richelieu are at once disqualified. Sheridan and Byron, too; for your true dandy had no velleity for letters. Brummell trifled with album verse, but could not stoop to poetry. All these men must go, with the dandy's crumpled cravats, into the basketful of "our failures." They failed because they were too complex: the dandy had the strength of ten of these because his strength was pure—pure dandyism. There is the test of your true dandy. Take away his dandyism and nothing remains. He represented the dandiacal idea, as Elia said Munden understood a leg of mutton, in its quiddity. What is this quiddity? Professor Teufelsdröckh found it in a clothes-horse. Vulgar error! A Spencer remained a dandy, shorn of one coat-tail. The dandy survived in Robert Macaire, though time and the hour had converted his gloves into mittens. It was the dandy who made the tailor, not the tailor the dandy. "I remember a Mr. Bosbury, a cutter of coats," says Beau Austin. "I have the vanity to believe I formed his business." Teufelsdröckh finds in the dandy the

apostle of a sect. The dandy as hot-gospeller—
faugh! And yet the dandy had a mission. It was
to vindicate the claims of caprice in an age of convention. It was to unsettle the complacent burgess
mind with the aleatory, to shock it with the unexpected. It was to spiritualize the mode. It was
to codify the laws of frivolity. It was to re-arrange
the social hierarchy, to make wealth, rank, intellect
yield precedence to elegance. Even more than a
missionary was the dandy an artist. *Anch' io son
pittore*, he might have boasted, had he condescended
to the lingo of fiddlers. He was his own paint and
canvas, and pleased with his person as other men
with their works. And he interpreted his own ideas,
not other men's. Hence in the scale of merit he
ranks above the great actor. Lastly, he was a
philosopher. For he made something out of naught,
proved that the superfluous is the necessary, and,
generally, that nothing is but thinking makes it so.
Your true dandy was your truest idealist.

This is the analysis of the late-Georgian dandy.
My sufficient excuse for working it out here is that it
is the true key to the dramatic synthesis of him
attempted in *Beau Austin*. And there remains yet
another indispensable preliminary to the proper comprehension of the play in the answer to the question:
What were the dandy's relations to women? Of
course he was no professional Don Juan. Passion
would have been fatal to a starched cravat. Seduc-
tion, as a finishing touch to elegance, a *bravura* piece
of virtuosity in the art of life, could not be wholly
dispensed with; but it was a mere parergon. This
sultan had higher uses for his cambric handkerchief
than to throw it. It was for him what Hilmar
Tönnesen calls a banner of the ideal, not a missile.

But the sultanas all snatched it. "Not to pine for that Sylvander," says Miss Foster of George Austin, "was to resign from good society." As for marriage, his quasi-royal position put that out of the question. Hear Miss Foster once more. "The attentions of a gentleman like Mr. Austin are not supposed to lead to matrimony. A private gentleman by birth, but a kind of king by habit and reputation, what woman could he marry? Those to whom he might properly aspire are all too far below him. The very greatness of his success compels him to remain unmarried."

It is here that we first put the play to the touch. The authors of *Beau Austin* undertake to achieve the impossible, to induce their dandy to marry. Well and good. That is a gallant adventure. But they do not storm their stronghold: it surrenders without a siege or so much as a sortie. In an act and a-half they have planted their dandy firmly upon his legs. What manner of man he is has been skilfully revealed in the enthusiasm of Miss Foster (she had walked her first minuet with him about the time of Nelson and the Nile, when "he had killed his man, wore pink and silver, was most elegantly pale, and the most ravishing creature"); and a scene between the Beau and his valet, close followed by one between the great man and a pert Tom-and-Jerry youth, Anthony Musgrave, nephew to Miss Foster and cornet in Austin's old regiment, the "Prince's Own," completes the synthesis of the dandy. We have already learned—what Anthony as yet has not—that his sister Dorothy had some six months ago become one of the sultanas. Her old sweetheart, John Fenwick, has learned it too, and from her own lips. Fenwick at once seeks an interview with the Beau, and appeals to his generosity. Surely this should be the *scène-à-faire* of the piece;

for is it not " one of the passionate *cruces* of life where duty and inclination come nobly to the grapple "? But this grapple turns out suspiciously like some modern grapples of another sort: grapples managed "on the cross," where the spectator gets barely a single round for his money. The Beau pleads that a dandy should not be asked to be Quixotic. If he had married every lady by whom it was his fortune to have been distinguished, the Wells would scarce be spacious enough for his establishment. In the duel of sex the lady had been winged, and there was an end of it. But, finding Fenwick persistent, the Beau gives in without more ado. His age, he says (he is fifty), makes him clement. His is now the royal mood of the mature man: to abdicate for others. He will marry Dorothy. Thus one brief scene suffices to resolve a situation which it takes the author of *Denise* five whole acts to work out. Not a doubt of it, this *scène-à-faire*, to speak once more the Sarceian dialect, is *escamotée*. If I held a brief for the authors, which I do not, I should answer that Sarcey and Dumas have nothing to do with the matter, that this play is sampler-work, and that the sampler, like the willow-pattern plate, has its own laws, or rather its own anarchies, of perspective. I am not of those who are disposed to find fault with the ensuing situation of the play, Dorothy's refusal of the Beau's offer. That seems to me, in Mr. Ruskin's phrase, entirely right. In the first place for the very sufficient reason that, without it, there would be an end of the play. The game would be up. And Dorothy's answer is not only necessary in the play but natural in life. The Beau's offer is six months too late. It is not spontaneous; it forces upon her a humiliating alternative: " Marry me, or you are dishonoured; marry me, or your brother " (for Anthony has learnt all and is vowing vengeance) "dies." No. To blame the Beau for capitulating too soon, and the lady for not capitulating soon enough, is to strain the privileges of critical inconsistency.

To demand that the lady should persist in her rejection would show a morbid taste for "unhappy endings" or the Ibsenite "note of interrogation." At all costs Beau Austin must be saved from following Brummell into exile at Calais. And to have preceded Prince Florizel of Bohemia (the Beau's descendant, I am sure, by one of the other sultanas) into the retirement of a Leicester Square cigar divan would have been too great a concession in an age of snuff. Accordingly, after the Beau has passed through the crucible of martyrdom by enduring, without retaliation, a blow in the face from the infuriated Anthony in the presence of a royal duke, and has emerged singed but purified, Dorothy rushes into his arms. When the curtain has fallen upon the dandy's magnificent "Your Royal Highness, may I present you Mrs. George Frederick Austin?" George doubtless turns to his new brother-in-law with an anticipation of M. Augier's "*Efface!*" The royal duke, by the way, is a *persona muta*. Learn that royalty in the presence of a dandy, like the æsthete in presence of a Botticelli, is dumb. But Lord Burleigh's nod is a dangerous experiment to try twice.

It was not without design that I alluded to Prince Florizel. All the characters (except Anthony, *cui contigit adire Corinthum*) speak the stately speech of that great and good man : Miss Leclercq perhaps with more orotund fervour than her comrades. Though I checked the players by the book, I never once detected a slip from the elegant idiom of 1820 to the canonised slang of 1890. Indeed, the dialogue throughout was music to the ear, and each dress a separate ecstasy for the eye: the whole atmosphere of the play reproduced the subtle aroma of the age of the dandies. Mr. Tree's was the hardest task. He had to recapture the fugitive graces of a Brummell: and the dandy belongs to the category of the actor, the orator, the talker—types *qui parlent* (in Buffon's phrase) *au corps par le corps*, of all types the most difficult to reproduce. Mr. Tree nearly mastered the difficulty, and would have quite mastered it had he padded out his dandy with a little more regal magnificence and moderated his transports of lachrymose sentiment. Your dandy, to be sure, was born to invent new trimmings for his sleeves, but I do not think it would ever have occurred to him to wear his heart there. Mrs. Tree played with quiet, somewhat too quiet, dignity; Mr. Edmund Maurice was excellent as the Corinthian hobbledehoy, getting into the very skin of the part; and Mr. Brookfield, a master of "stipple" in art, "composed" the valet with all his usual skill, and more. One little weakness in the valet distresses me, and that is not Mr. Brookfield's. The man is, of course, the *replica* (in jean) of the dandy. " He has the beau's own walk to that degree you can't tell his back from his master's." But the imitation is carried one step too far. When the master capitulates, the man approves. I cannot forgive him for this. He should have been more royalist than the king: the stern, unbending devotee of dandyism left alone to mourn his " lost leader." When Austin bids him "get out the tongs, and curl me like a bridegroom," he should have given notice on the spot.

HENRY ARTHUR JONES.

ON PLAY-MAKING.

"THE theatre is irresistible; organize the theatre."
I comforted myself with these words of Matthew Arnold as I sate gasping for air one Sunday night in a little hall just out of Oxford Street, which was so densely packed with more or less human beings (for the audience included several squalling infants) that the Black Hole of Calcutta must have seemed by comparison a spacious and well-ventilated apartment. Squeezed ribs and a battered hat were for me the best evidence that "the theatre is irresistible." Sunday night is the one night in the week that you can't go to the theatre; so here were all these people doing something else, listening to a lecture about it, getting themselves "organized" for it. For before you can organize your theatre, you must organize your audience, teach them to have a theory, a policy, and a plan—like Popkins. Much has been done in this way by the Playgoers' Club, with its apparatus of discussions, dinners, picnics, smoking-concerts, pamphlets, and what not. And something, too, has been done by these lectures on the drama, arranged by the National Sunday League and kindred societies. On this particular Sunday the lecturer was Mr. Henry Arthur Jones, who discoursed of "Play-making," with especial reference to "plot, design, and construction."

The latest tendency of theatrical opinion makes against construction. A distinct reaction has set in against the "well-made" piece, invented by Scribe and perfected by Sardou. Two of the most successful plays of the season on either side of the Channel, *Paris Fin de Siècle* and *The Cabinet Minister*, both of them openly and contemptuously ignored the orthodox rules of construction; in each case the plot was no plot, but a mere string on which character sketches were hung in a row. The advantage to the diner-out, and to the congenitally unpunctual, was immense. You turned into the Gymnase or the Court at any hour, sure of finding some amusing incident in progress, something which demanded no knowledge of what had gone before or of what was to follow. On purely material grounds, therefore—the late dinner-hour of modern man, and his incapacity, after dinner, for sustained attention—we may predict the doom of dramatic construction. But this, I hasten to warn you, is my grovelling explanation of the matter, not Mr. Henry Arthur Jones's. He, in his quality of Sunday lecturer, naturally had to take a more serious, a more artistic view. "Story and incident and situation," said he, "are, unless related to the character, comparatively childish and unintellectual. They should be only another aspect of the development of character. . . . Where construction is made of the first importance—where neatness and perfection of construction are obtained, it is generally at the cost of truthfulness and force and subtlety of character. . . . The moment the construction of a play becomes so ingenious as to be noticeable, at that moment it passes its limits, and convicts the playwright of an attempt not to paint human nature, but to show his own cleverness. That construction, then, is the best which sinks itself and is entirely unobtrusive, and moves quite silently and unnoticed under the truths of character and life which the dramatist has to present." And, finally, to sum up, "I want you to remember that the plot and story and construction should be inferior to the truthful exhibition of life and character. I wish you to be discontented with all merely ingenious construction, all that savours of artifice and trick."

The gist of these remarks seem to me to be: Take care of your characters, and your plot will take care of itself. Excellent, so far as it goes! But there are some temerarious spirits who go a step farther than Mr. Jones. Nature, say these, shows no plot, design, construction, at all; why then should the drama, whose function it is to hold the mirror up to nature? "The strange irregular rhythm of life" (as Mr. Henry James puts it), that is what the uncompromising realists want the drama to imitate. Mr. Jones cannot abide these realists. "The stage is not real life," he said, amid the loud applause of his audience. "Those people who want real life can go into the streets and get it." Is not Mr. Jones a little too cock-sure about this? At any rate, the illustration which he chose for the enforcement of his proposition is demonstrably false. Life, said he, supplies the raw material for the drama, as the hillside on which a cathedral is raised supplies the stone for its building. It was a sort of rule of three sum :—

Drama : Life : : Cathedral : Quarry.

"There should be design in every portion of the cathedral. But it was all hewn from the surrounding hillside." *Ergo*, drama should have the design which life has not.

Curiously enough, I find this very illustration anticipated for the same purpose more than a century ago (to be precise, about 1765) by Burke in his little-known and fragmentary "Hints for an Essay on the Drama." "We may as well urge that stones, sand, clay, and metals lie in a certain manner in the earth, as a reason for building with these materials and in that manner, as for writing according to the accidental disposition of character in nature." A moment's reflection ought to show that this illustration of Burke's and Mr. Jones's is essentially false and misleading, for the simple reason that architecture is not, like the drama, an imitative art. Life is not only the raw material for the stage, it is the model as well. True, you cannot transfer life to the stage in its integrity: limitations of time and space forbid that; there must be selection, arrangement, concentration. But, even with selection, "the strange irregular rhythm of life" might be imitated. The ultra-realists have a better case than Mr. Jones suspects.

On the whole, the lecture left one with the impression that Mr. Jones, earnest and enlightened reformer though he is, might have gone further and fared no worse. He has not unlearned all the old dogmatic criticism. He relegates construction to a back seat, but he shrinks from showing it the door. And, in the matter of ethics, he is still one of the old apostles who preach that there are things not convenient for the stage. He has not yet cast out the devil (Pickwickianly speaking) of Ruskinism. Art must be "healthy." The drama must not study vice, disease, the disagreeable, the ugly. I venture, quite respectfully, to suggest that a course of M. Antoine and the *Théâtre Libre* would do Mr. Jones a world of good. It would, I trust, convince him that the hope of a great future for the stage lies in perfect freedom : freedom to try every kind of experiment ; freedom to be realistic or idealistic, prosaic or fantastic, "well-made" or plotless, "healthy" or pathological ; freedom to go anywhere, like the British Army, and do anything. Meanwhile, let us be grateful to him for the valuable service he is rendering to the drama by expounding its mysteries to the multitude. But, oh, my poor ribs!

"THE MIDDLEMAN."

(*Shaftesbury Theatre, August*, 1889.)

IT is astute of Mr. Jones to claim for his recent plays that they are in intention serious studies of modern social and commercial life. The claim whets public curiosity at a time when sociology is being brought home to all our doors, and economics are served up hot with the morning muffin. It excites a little flutter of expectation among a considerable number of guileless playgoers, who are led to suppose that here at last is a dramatist who means to throw the searching glare of the footlights upon the laws of wealth distribution, capital and labour, supply and demand, and other high matters. But Mr. Jones's claim, when brought to the proof, breaks down. *The Middleman!* What an attractive bait for the pale student of Mill and Jevons! How his mouth must water at the anticipation of some quite novel dramatic experiment; a play (he will, of course, surmise) of three protagonists—producer, consumer, and middleman—the last, of course, to be the villain of the piece, argued out of his life by the other two, and finally chased off the stage as an economic parasite! His anticipation, as need hardly be said to those who know what the stage can do and what it cannot, will find no fulfilment in Mr. Jones's play. The Shaftesbury "middleman" is so, as it were, merely by accident. To be sure, he has something to say about the advantage to the community of men whose enterprise puts the production of others into commercial circulation. But this *apologia* for his function is mere embroidery. It is not his commercial function that is of dramatic significance in the play; it is his situation as a father who will not permit his son to marry the woman whom he, the son, has dishonoured. For the rest, he is a mere purse-proud manufacturer of the conventional stage type, intriguing to get into Parliament, into county society, and so forth—in a word, M. Ohnet's Moulinet over again. Is it, then, in the character of the inventor, upon whom the middleman battens, that we are to seek Mr. Jones's study of actual life? We all know the type of modern inventor—a Pasteur, an Eiffel, an Edison. Has Mr. Jones tried to realize this type for us on the stage? Not a bit of it. His inventor is of the old, old footlight sort: an unpractical, dazed, almost demented dreamer—the sort that Augier drew in the Desroncerets of *Maître Guérin*, and Tom Taylor, in the Peter Hayes of *Arkwright's Wife*. Such inventors have existed, and still exist, no doubt; but they are not the typical inventors of to-day. I must, then, respectfully decline Mr. Jones's invitation to accept his play as a piece of actuality. I prefer to recognize its merits as a piece of frank romance. Mr. Jones has shown the true theatrical instinct in making his inventor here a potter. The dramatic element of surprise, chased by machinery out of the other industrial arts, still clings to this art of pottery. Just think of it. You put a more or less amorphous lump of ugly clay into the mouth of a blazing furnace. You wait wearily, anxiously, for days, knowing that on what shall issue from that furnace hangs fortune or ruin.

Perhaps the furnace burns low, and you have no more money to buy fuel. Then you make a holocaust of your furniture and feed the flames with chair-legs and the kitchen dresser. All this is highly romantic, nay, necromantic. It has the glamour of the old alchemy. At last the furnace cools. You tear away the bricks, and take out the ware. Horror! It has crumbled to dust. Stay, what is this? One piece has survived, to show you have discovered the grand secret. You have transmuted base metal into gold, and the world lies at your feet. Of course this scene is the great scene of Mr. Jones's play. But it is not the world that Cyrus Blenkarn, the old inventor, wants at his feet; it is his old enemy, the "middleman," who has refused to let his son "make an honest woman" of the inventor's daughter, and has thereby, it is thought, driven her to her grave. The discovery of the new glaze puts revenge into Cyrus's power; his old enemy, beggared by the success of a ware that drives his own out of the market, becomes (very literally) like clay in the hands of the potter. But at the last moment, just as he is taking possession of the bankrupt middleman's house, his wrath is stayed by the return home of the son with the daughter not only restored to life, but (I do not profess to understand how or where the marriage has taken place) a blushing bride into the bargain.

"JUDAH."

(Shaftesbury Theatre, May, 1890.)

"LACHEZ l'admirable," they said to Théophile Gautier, as he sat biting his pen over his "copy" after a great Parisian success, and I, too, am tempted to "let go the admirable" over *Judah*. But I bethink me in time that it is not the critic's function to be a singer of pæans. The critic's apartment in that House Beautiful of which he is the Interpreter is not a larder of butter-tubs, but an analytical laboratory. That I am pleased with the play is not the point. The real question is, Why am I pleased?

Putting my pleasure, then, in the chemist's phrase, into solution, I get, in the last analysis, this precipitate: an æsthetic gratification arising from the contrast between the vulgarity of subject of the new play and the nobility of its treatment. In the whole history of imposture there are no chapters more sordid and sorry to read than those headed "Faith-healing" and "Fasting-girls." The associations of quackery, cheap thaumaturgy, Aquarium exhibitions, police-court prosecutions, and coroners' inquests that cling around these two things—faugh! one sickens to think of them. One shudders, too, to think what the mechanical melodramatist would make of such subjects, of his five-act game of hide-and-seek between wicked mediums and Gaboriau-detectives. Well, the author of *Judah* has touched these vulgarities, and straightway has transfigured them. He has spiritualized them, woven round them a soul-tragedy, turned their common homespun into a web shot with the iridescent lights of conscience, mental agony, moral struggle, fall, and redemption.

Vashti Dethic is the faith-healing, fasting-girl. Her father is the Sludge of the story. The pair gain a footing in the house of the Earl of Asgarby by undertaking to cure his consumptive daughter, Lady Eve. Coerced by her father, Vashti accepts the challenge of a scientific sceptic, Professor Jopp, to fast under strict surveillance. The father gets a duplicate key to the daughter's guarded chamber, and tries to run the blockade with food. There is a scene—a discovery being averted by a hair's-breadth, household roused at dead of night, ringing of alarm bells, and so forth— but stop, some one says, is not all this sort of thing just the very mechanical melodrama you spoke of? There is, perhaps, a faint touch of the mechanical melodramatist in the contrivance of the scene in question : in the blindman's buff played by various couples in evening dress round the door of Vashti's prison-house. But it is only a faint touch. The interest here does not lie in the mechanism. It lies in the spiritual drama of Vashti's position. She has won the love of a good man, and is only induced to keep up her imposture by the fear that the disclosure of her real self would mean the loss of that love. The fear turns out to be groundless. Her lover—Judah Llewellyn, a Welsh Presbyterian minister with a strain of Jewish blood and the gift of tongues of a Minor Prophet— discovers that Vashti is a cheat. But he still clings to his shattered idol, and sacrifices his own honour on her shrine. Indeed, this Welsh Minor Prophet—like that other Minor Prophet, Habbakuk, as described by Voltaire—is *capable de tout*. When taxed point-blank by the scientific sceptic, he saves Vashti by taking his oath to a lie. With his belief in Vashti, his belief in faith-healing, in faith itself, is gone, and he feels his own probity may go too. Therefore, he shields his love with a lie, a good thumping lie. On this strong —spiritually strong, observe, not merely mechanically strong—situation the curtain of the second act falls.

The third act is all pure, unadulterated, spiritual drama; the drama of the minister, venerated by his flock, on the point of being endowed with a brand-new church and a brand-new testimonial, tormented by the continual word "liar!" which he hears at every moment as Mathias hears the jingle of the sleigh-bells. But at last he frees his soul, as Consul Bernick frees his, and as Arthur Dimmesdale frees his. At the supreme moment of outward triumph, when all the town is gathered together to present him with the testimonial and the deeds of the new church, he confesses himself the liar that he is, and induces Vashti to confess with him. Shall they go, or stay? Stay, say the neighbours, and work out your redemption among your old flock and friends. The resemblance of this final situation to that of the *Pillars of Society* is, of course, obvious.

Indeed, something of the Ibsen spirit seems to me to pervade the play; it breathes in the discussion of the *pros* and *cons* of spiritualism *v.* materialism in the first act; one detects it again in the final oath-breaking situation of the second: it is the very essence of the remorse and sacrifice of the third. The serious drama is lightened by some admirable comedy scenes, scenes of a freshness, originality, modernity, quite remarkable. These are partly supplied by the queer courtship of a couple of highly cultivated, cynical, pedantic lovers, partly by some sharp passages at arms between Professor Jopp and Sludge the medium—I mean Dethic. Of the young lovers I will only say that such comic wooing between prig and blue-stocking has not been seen on the stage since Pailleron wrote the interview between Bellac and Lucy in the third act of *Le Monde où l'on s'Ennuie.*

THE REALIST IN SPITE OF HIMSELF.

(May, 1890.)

I AM sorry that Mr. Jones should have chosen the present moment to run a-tilt against stage realism. Here is a man who, on the morrow of writing a play far truer, stronger, sincerer than his other plays precisely because it is more realistic, asks us to reject stage realism as contemptible and untrue ! M. Jourdain, as we are reminded on an average about a dozen times a week, spoke prose without knowing it, but he at least refrained from pouring contempt on the prose he unconsciously used. The outcry against realism usually proceeds from the stupid and Philistine, from the people who take their ideas at second-hand, who have never been at the pains clearly to understand what realism is. With them the word has vague associations of Holywell Street, Jan Van Beers' pictures, and a general sense of naughtiness. To find one of our very foremost dramatists in such company is a thing young Mr. Juxon Prall would call deplorable. Mr. Jones appears to have a somewhat hazy notion of what realism is. He thinks it is something opposed to truth. He says the uneducated play-goer " knows no difference between realism and truth." Does, then, Mr. Jones know any ? Does he imagine this to be a sound antithesis ?

Mr. Jones should consult his friend Professor Jopp,

F.R.S., about the true inwardness of realism. The Professor will tell him that it is the attempt of art—under the impulse of an age affected by the scientific spirit—to obtain a closer approximation to the truth. It is the result of the Positivist spirit working in the region of art; it is based on the conquests of modern science, and especially on the theory of evolution. It is rooted in no dogma, no *à priori* notions, but in the study of nature, in observation, in experience : it admits only ascertained facts and the laws which express the relations between these facts. It exhibits the organism as conditioned by the environment, character as the resultant of circumstances, law reigning universally in the spiritual as in the material world, the sequence of cause and effect unbroken by any harlequin's wand. Like Professor Jopp, it does not believe in miracles. It expels the phœnix, the unicorn, and the jabberwock from the stage menagerie. These are well-worn commonplaces; my sufficient excuse for repeating them is that Mr. Jones entirely ignores them. Having falsely imagined realism to be something opposed to truth, he next falsely imagines it to be something hostile to every kind of stage convention. Now there are, of course, some fundamental conventions without which the art of the stage simply could not exist, *e.g.*, to name one out of many, the convention by which events happening in various places and over an extended period are represented actually in one place (the stage) and in a limited time (about three hours). "The realist," says Mr. Jones, "has to accept this monstrous convention to start with ; and having accepted it, why should he hesitate to accept a host of minor conventions, provided that they advance the dramatist's main business, the exposition and interpretation of human life and character?" Why, indeed? But what realist ever has so hesitated? The conventions the realist rejects are not those which advance, but those which impede, the exposition of human character—conventions which are the outcome of a false morality, of life seen through rose-coloured spectacles. These make virtue always sympathetic and vice always repugnant, contrive miraculous conversions in the last act, and reward honest poverty by the arrival of a rich uncle from America. These conventions gather grapes of thorns and figs of thistles, and these are the conventions which the realist "hesitates to accept."

"But," says Mr. Jones, "the rejection of stage realism is not antagonistic to the most severe, the most faithful, the most searching, the most truthful portraiture of modern life." In disproof of this, I appeal from Mr. Jones the critic to Mr. Jones the playwright. Let us take his three last plays in order, *Wealth, The Middleman*, and *Judah*, and I think it will not be difficult to show that the portraiture of modern life in each is least truthful precisely where there is most convention, where the rejection of stage realism has been most complete. In *Wealth* the comic personages on the one hand, the villain on the other, are figures of pure convention. The comic personages are a crowd of needy, avaricious relatives who surround the rich man of the play, and are always cadging for presents. Or, rather, they are not so much a crowd as a trained band, drilled to execute the manœuvre of coming on and off the stage together, to shout expostulations in unison, or to cajole the old man in single file. Is this a truthful portraiture of real life? No; it is the galvanization of a defunct tradition at least as old as the Elizabethan stage, *e.g.*, Ben Jonson's *Volpone*. The villain, the old man's nephew and partner, is all black; there is not one redeeming feature in him; he is always luring the old man to his ruin. Is this a truthful portraiture of the modern commercial man? Or is it Mephistopheles, without the cloven foot, the cock's feather, and the red fire?

In *The Middleman* the comic personages are a pair of lovers. For three acts the youth is at the maiden's beck-and-call and worships the ground she treads on, plays the slave to her tyrant. In the fourth the tables are turned by marriage — the youth becomes the domestic tyrant, the girl becomes the slave. Is this a truthful portraiture of modern life! Are modern lovers built like that? The realist "hesitates to accept" such trick-changes. The middleman himself is an embodiment of all the vices of the capitalist: insolent, purse-proud, a grinder of the faces of the poor. He even steals his daughter's letters. Here, again, there is no redeeming feature, no subtlety. In real life a baby would see through such an impostor. Is this a truthful portraiture of a modern capitalist? Or is it a symbolical figure from a *Punch* cartoon? Mr. Jones will answer that he has made this figure monochromatic, and all of a piece, because in art you must simplify, select, exaggerate. But the realist will ask, would not this simplification have been obtained without all sacrifice of respect for the complexity of life and human character? Would not the artistic effect have been increased tenfold if the middleman had displayed some of the virtues of the capitalist as well as all the vices, if those vices had been shown to be the natural outcome of circumstances—amongst others, of a morbid economic condition? It so happens that another dramatist has treated this same subject, long before Mr. Jones handled it. Augier's Maître Guérin makes a fortune by swindling a simple-minded inventor. The man is a rogue, but he is a complex rogue. It comes as natural to him to get the better of a simpleton as to any other bird-of-prey to be a bird-of-prey. He has throughout a certain genial humour, a rude common sense, even a rough philosophy and sense of justice ("All's fair in love and war"— "Every man for himself, and the devil take," &c.). At the last, when he finds the world turn against him, he is honestly indignant; he has acted in good faith, according to his nature; *he does not understand*. There you have realism; there you have simplification which respects the complexity of human character; there you have truthful portraiture of modern life.

Now turn to *Judah*, and see how far ahead that is of the two other plays, because of its advance in the direction of that very realism which Mr. Jones calls contemptible. Observe that for the first time the comic personages have become realistic. The lovers, Juxon Prall and Miss Jopp, are not merely modern; they are "end of the century." It was only the other day that the author of "The Kreutzer Sonata" pleaded for marriage with the physical element eliminated, and based on intellectual affinity. Mr. Jones's two lovers who get betrothed without a kiss, and find their sympathy in identity of views about Darwin, present the comic side of Tolstoy's notion. I know both these young people. Miss Jopp has come straight out of Girton. As for Juxon Prall, the young man who snubs his mamma for her bad logic and cannot forgive his papa's heterodox views on Protection and Bimetallism, have we not all met him? Have we not argued with him on the Underground Railway, and found him occupying our favourite arm-chair at the club? He is a prig for whom, in a more literal sense than for Burke, "the age of chivalry is gone";

when the lady of his affections hints she would like to sit down, he says he doesn't see the necessity; he calmly discusses with her the prospect of a future family. This is realism, and very good realism. And it is just where realism is rejected that *Judah* becomes weakest. I will confess that I never knew the consumptive daughter of an earl, but I don't believe that these young ladies recite long dreams with impassioned eloquence to the company assembled in the drawing-room. But, remembering the *Silver King*, I do know that Mr. Jones has a foible for dream-speeches—they give him an opportunity for airing his talent for high-falutin' prose, and they provide the actor or actress with what is vulgarly known on the boards as a "bit of fat"—and so the consumptive daughter of the earl is made to recite a *bravura* passage about her dream. Good-bye to realism here, and good-bye along with it to truthful portraiture of modern life! The earl is a mere lay-figure; his grief over his daughter's consumption leaves one quite cold. Nor is the villain, Dethic, realistic enough to convince me of his existence. He is unexplained, an uncaused, unrelated phenomenon. One feels that he has been supplied to order: an automatic villain who only works because Mr. Jones has dropped a penny in the slot. Compare with him another villain, who comes naturally to my mind because he has been played by the same actor, Mr. Royce Carleton—I mean Ibsen's Krogstad. Krogstad was explained: one felt he *must* have been what he was; and that, but for luck, one might have been in his place. Now, conscious though I am of an infinite potentiality for turpitude, I cannot fancy myself exchanging places with Mr. Dethic. Fortunately, Dethic, the earl, and the earl's daughter, the unrealistic personages of the play,

THE REALIST IN SPITE OF HIMSELF.

are all unimportant. The chief figures of the play, Judah and Vashti, act according to the law of their natures, not according to the law laid down for hero and heroine by stage conventions; they are observed, alive—in short, realistic. Professor Jopp is realistic. The comic lovers, as I have said, are ultra-realistic. In sum, the author of *Judah* has achieved an artistic success because he has learnt to be a realist. It is one of the piquant ironies of life to discover in the man who calls realism contemptible a realist *malgré lui*.

"THE DANCING GIRL."

(Haymarket Theatre, January, 1891.)

THE mediæval hope that the old pagan gods are not dead but still survive, the "hillside men" of some Venusburg, or inhabiting the island of Heine's fancy, still lingers among us moderns, not as folk-lore, but in novels and plays. In vain have we "got religion," the Ten Commandments, conviction of sin, and chimney-pot hats; we yearn for the Athens of Pericles, the Greek cult of beauty, the Greek Joy of Living, *rêvant*, as M. Paul Verlaine sings, "*du divin Platon, et de Phidias, . . . sous l'œil clignotant des bleus becs de gaz*"—in Piccadilly. So we call ourselves Neo-Hellenists, and go up and down buying first editions of Mr. Pater. But this kind cometh not but with prayer and fasting, the reading of many books (and the first editions are expensive), together with a good deal of Mr. Richard Swiveller's "make-believe." Even then our modern Julians fail; the Galilean has conquered. But where we, with all our striving, fail, Nature sometimes succeeds. Now and again (if we are to believe the novelists and dramatists) a woman —it is generally a woman, the Eternal Feminine having the best of the luck, as usual—reincarnates for us the pure Pagan type. She is a creature of surpassing beauty, a tinted Venus, as Mr. Anstey would say, and she has no conscience, no moral sense—that is, she is not immoral, but non-moral. Whether her birth squares with the law of heredity or not is quite a toss-up. Becky Sharp's did, for Becky was the daughter of a drunken artist and a French *ballerina*. Regina Engstrand, too, took after her mother. But sometimes what the biologists call " sports " occur. Nature reverts to the ancient type capriciously, and grows figs from thistles. That is the case with Drusilla Ives, the latest feminine reincarnation of Paganism, and the heroine of Mr. Jones's new play, *The Dancing Girl*. This tinted Venus is a harmony in white and grey. I mean that Drusilla is the daughter of a Quaker family, who inhabit the Cornish island of St. Endellion, an island peopled entirely by Quakers— Quakers tempered by harmoniums. Here we find the Neo-Pagan Quakeress, demurely clad, "thee"-ing and "thou"-ing her kinsfolk, and, the moment their backs are turned, taking off her slipper to show her shapely foot to one man, or practising a "shadow-dance" for the delectation of another.

The fact is, they do not know everything down in St. Endellion. They do not know, for instance, that the "Christian" situation in which their Drusilla is supposed to have been serving up in London has been really of a "Corybantic" nature, that she has fascinated "smart" society in the character of Diana Valrose, "the dancing girl," and become the paramour of his Scapegrace the Duke of Guisebury. The duke is a neo-Pagan like his mistress—a Pagan, however, who has dipped into the Upanishads and is troubled, as his mistress is not, with obstinate questionings of invisible things. His philosophic bias, by the way, has not prevented him from wasting his substance in riotous living, or *The Trafalgar Square Gazette* from declaring that "the spectacle of his career has shortened the future of the House of Lords by twenty years." It is for his enjoyment (he is landlord of St. Endellion and on a visit to the island) that the shadow-dance is rehearsed; and the dismay of a St. Edellionite, interrupting the little performance with a thundering, "Woman, what art thou?" provides what stage-managers call a "good curtain" for the first act.

In the second, the dramatist's conception of the character of Drusilla is more fully developed. The modest Quaker garb has now been thrown off; she has exchanged the fig-leaf for the strawberry leaf, or, to vary the metaphor, the lilies and languor of St. Endellion for the roses and rapture of a ducal villa at Richmond. But already the roses are crumpled. The duke is ruined by the extravagance of his mistress, who, a true devotee of the Joy of Living, is beginning to find an impecunious lover a bore. In desperation he offers her his coronet, which she coldly refuses. Then merely by way of pastime she exercises her fascinations upon a Quaker sweetheart, until he takes his courage in both hands and flees.

Throughout, the woman's character is consistently and firmly drawn: she is heartless, unconsciously cruel, fated to be a noxious thing to every man within her spell, what M. Dumas *fils* used to call *la bête*. It is a novel type on an English stage, and the dramatist has depicted it with consummate skill. I do not think he has been so successful with his duke. This duke philosophizes too much. The shibboleth of pessimism comes too glibly off his tougue (he even confides Schopenhauerisms to the crop-ears of his bull-dog), he patters too freely about "Nirvana," is altogether too pedantic to carry conviction. As a reader of *The Nineteenth Century*, I know that some dukes are pedants, but I do not associate them with dancing girls. I associate this one, rather—may Mr. Jones forgive me!—with the pages of Ouida. His bull-dog is Ouidaesque; his headlong extravagance is Ouidaesque; his pseudo-philosophy is Ouidaesque; he has even rescued a lady from under the hoofs of runaway horses—which is right Ouidaesque.

It is in the third act that this rescued lady shows us the real reason why she was snatched from an untimely death. The dramatist wanted her for the crisis of his play. We have had glimpses of her in the first two acts, through which she has flitted, a little cripple, half sad, half merry, acting as fairy godmother to the duke's tenantry, and as a sort of outspoken Miss-Mowcher-like monitress to the duke himself. When such an apparently superfluous character as this appears in the earlier stages of a play, the experienced play-goer at once knows what to expect. He says to himself, "You are useless now, therefore your turn will come by and by; it's no use deceiving me—I know you—your real name is *Dénouement*." And so it is here. The duke (his allusions to "Nirvana" in the preceding act were too significant to be missed) has determined to die, and, like Sardanapalus, he will die amid a general conflagration—that is, at the close of a magnificent entertainment, where all "smart" society shall be gathered together to applaud the "dancing girl," and to admire the strange arras made specially for the occasion out of "the funeral trappings of the Emperor of China" (Ouida again!— or is it Victor Hugo?). The evolutions of the fashionable crowd in this scene are a marvel of stage-management; the Meiningers could not have manœuvred better. In the height of the festivity, Drusilla's father appears, tears the finery off the girl's back, and "smart" society, scandalized, rushes out pell-mell, leaving the duke to turn down the gas and take his plunge into Nirvana alone. Then comes the turn of the rescued lady, Miss Dénouement, who steals up to the duke and snatches the poison-phial from his hand as the curtain descends. The scene passes in dead silence, and is one of those triumphs of theatrical effect which reveal the born dramatist.

Up to this point the play has never once lost its grip of the audience, and if only it could end here (why not, Mr. Jones? Why not take a hint from the third act of *Ghosts ?*) all would be well. But there is, unfortunately, a fourth act—a fourth act as weak as the preceding three are strong. We are back in St. Endellion, among the Quakers and harmoniums. Drusilla is dead. The duke is reformed, and (cruel penance for a Schopenhauerite and Anglo-Buddhist) lets Miss Dénouement, whom he is on the point of marrying, quote Herbert Spencer to him by the yard. After marriage, no doubt, she will read him whole chapters from "In Darkest England." But before that dire consummation is reached, the curtain, luckily, descends.

TERENCE, LABICHE, AND SYDNEY GRUNDY.

"A PAIR OF SPECTACLES."

(Garrick Theatre, May, 1890.)

A TRUE comedy played by true comedians. To help you to its clear comprehension and full enjoyment, let me ask you to follow me in a little historical retrospect. My only difficulty is at what point of history to begin, for the motive of this Garrick play is so old, so deep down in human nature, that there can be no doubt it was played in some form or other at the Court Theatres of Tiglath-Pilezer and Chedor-Laomer. But don't be alarmed. I will take you no further back than two thousand and fifty years —to B.C. 161. In that year, at the funeral games of Æmilius l'aulus, and at the expense of our old school friend, Scipio Africanus, was performed at Rome for the first time, the comedy of *The Brothers*, by Publius Terentius Afer. You were not among the audience; no more was I. But once in every four years you and I may still see this play performed within a mile of Charing Cross, by the boys of Westminster School.

Now let us take a big jump both of space and time, to London in 1688, among the dramatic novelties of which year Mr. John Downes, some time prompter of the Lincoln's-inn-fields Theatre, notes "*The Squire of*

Alsatia, a comedy wrote by Mr. Shadwell. This play, by its excellent acting, being often honoured by the presence of Chancellour Jefferies" (another old school friend), "had an uninterrupted run of thirteen days together." Shadwell's play is the *Adelphi* re-written.

Another jump, please. This time to the Vaudeville Theatre, Paris, April 1, 1862. On that date was produced the comedy of *Les Petits Oiseaux*, by MM. Eugène Labiche and A. Delacour. Thanks to the acting of Numa, Parade, and Saint-Germain, this comedy was a great success, and had to be repeated before the Emperor and Empress at Compiègne. Labiche's play is the *Adelphi* re-written.

Now we are at our last hurdle. The other night was produced at the Garrick the comedy, *A Pair of Spectacles*. Mr. Sydney Grundy, the adapter, in response to loud calls for the author, came forward and announced (without naming the original piece) that the authors were MM. Labiche and Delacour. Mr. Grundy's play is *Les Petits Oiseaux* re-written.

There's a respectable pedigree for you ! A play, in all essentials, over a thousand years old ! The fact is, the Pythagorean faith, however heterodox elsewhere, is gospel truth inside the playhouse. A dramatic soul never dies ; it only transmigrates. In this case you have the soul of Terence, after sojourning for a while in the bodies of Mr. Thomas Shadwell and M. Eugène Labiche, at length taking refuge in the manly bosom of Mr. Sydney Grundy.

The idea which has thus lived—like the Wandering Jew—through the ages, is simplicity itself. It is, I fear, an idea more consolatory than true. It may be described as a glove-fight between two philosophies: Optimism and Philanthropy *v*. Pessimism and Misanthropy. The pair have several terrific rounds, and, in the end, Pessimism is "knocked out" by Optimism. Moral : Excess of confidence is better than excess of mistrust ; there are still good people on this earth— worthy parents, honest tradesfolk, faithful friends ; in a word, the devil of humanity is not so black as he is painted. As a head-line for a copybook nothing could be better. But the ultra-realists will decline to swallow it, I suspect ; while Mr. George Moore and the other leopard-can't-change-his-spots philosophers will certainly rail.

For the leopards in this piece change their spots as easily as an American carpet-bagger changes his opinions. As quick-change artists they could give points to the chameleon. The fact is, the piece has no pretensions to realism ; it is too old for that. The two brothers, Benjamin and Gregory Goldfinch (the Demea and Micio of Terence, the two Belfonds of Shadwell, the Blandinet and François of Labiche)— Bunyan would have called them Mr. Trust and Mr. Distrust—are not real persons, but ideas personified. Trust lives at Hampstead ; believes in his banker because they were old schoolfellows ; in his lawyer because he knew his lawyer's father ; and lets his tenants off their rent because their wives are always (on quarter day) in an interesting condition. Distrust comes from Sheffield, only believes in what he sees, and preaches from the text, " Keep your eyes open and your pockets shut." Trust gets a begging-letter, which Distrust bets him will turn out a fraud. It does, and with the discovery Trust's whole nature changes. He comes to seeing everything through Distrust's spectacles, not merely metaphorically, but literally, for his own glasses being broken, he borrows a pair of his brother's. He now keeps all the keys, weighs the butcher's meat, measures the brandy in the decanter, and is even induced to suspect his innocent little wife's fidelity. Trust, in fact, has become another Distrust. Fortunately, the consequences of the report that he is ruined restore his faith in human nature. All his old friends rush to his aid; his old servants renounce their wages; his tenants hurry to him with their arrears of rent; he finds that the letters which had caused his suspicions of his wife are his own love-letters; and—miracle of miracles— Mr. Distrust from Sheffield offers his brother half his fortune. Curtain: and copybook moral as already given.

When Mr. Grundy disclaims all share in the authorship of *A Pair of Spectacles*, he sins from over-modesty. I have re-read Labiche's piece, and very good fun it is. But I venture to say Mr. Grundy's version is much better fun. To begin with, it is much purer fun. Mr. Grundy has made a clean sweep of the one disagreeable feature in the original—the suggestion of an intrigue between Trust's young wife and her husband's nephew. And he has added innumerable good things of his own. For instance, the idea of putting the dots on the i's by putting Distrust's spectacles (real not figurative) on Trust's nose is Grundy, not Labiche. The idea of the hidden packet of letters, which Trust thinks are from his wife's lover and finds to be from himself, is Grundy, not Labiche. Two points in the dialogue—one, when Trust in a violent outburst against the hardness of Distrust, rises in a *crescendo* of " You are "—everything that is detestable —" you are—you are—" (then, with a sudden drop of the voice) " *my brother* "; the other, when Trust, after scurrying out with the scales to weigh the cutlets brought by the butcher, comes back crestfallen, saying,

"They were *overweight*"—both these points are Grundy, not Labiche. Again, the spare but effective use of a text from a Bible which Trust finds in his wife's desk is Grundy, not Labiche. Some critic objects that this reference to a Bible on the stage is in questionable taste. Perhaps critics would not be the worse if they read their Bibles a little more and lip-reverenced them a little less. To me, at any rate, this use of the Bible seems not the least adroit of Mr. Grundy's interpolations. Trust is a character of simplicity quite Biblical, and the Scriptural text strikes just the right chord of deeper human feeling which is dumb in Labiche's play.

REVISITED.

A PAIR of Spectacles is a wholesome play. Between ourselves, I little thought to find myself using that abominable word, wholesome. It is the pet adjective of a fast vanishing school of English critics, the people who prate about the identity of the good, the beautiful, and the true. They darken counsel with it, and, lugging ethics into the domain of æsthetics, make criticism the abomination of desolation. From me, you will please take this compromising word as nothing more than the symptom of a passing mental state; it represents a reaction from an overdose of Zola. I have been reading "La Bête Humaine," and it has revolted me. As a rule, I can sup as full of horrors as the rest of my fellow citizens. Many an agreeable half hour have I spent at the Morgue, and the Chamber of Horrors in Baker Street is to me a Paradise of Dainty Devices. But the horrible mess of lust and blood, satyromania and homicidal epilepsy in this book of Zola's was too much for me. It laid me under the Hebraic commandment of being unclean until even. So I threw the thing away half-read, and betook me to the Garrick for a second look at *A Pair of Spectacles*.

The play proved, as I expected, an admirable disinfectant. The very scene, with its neat bookcases in white pine, its ample flower-decked bay window, its clean napery and breakfast equipage, was a sort of ablution. "Mr. Goldfinch's Morning Room at Hampstead"—the mere words were breezy with fresh air. And the entrance of Mr. Sydney Brough, perfect type of that young Englishman whom one always first thinks of as well-washed (by the way, this young actor had an uncle once known in the Bohemian world of letters as "clean Brough"— which was a poor compliment to another uncle) furthered a process of purification which the play itself completed. The triumph of optimism and philanthropy in the person of Mr. Benjamin Goldfinch, the vindication of his "Keep your pockets open and your eyes shut," the way in which all his family and friends end by turning his house into a veritable dairy of the milk of human kindness—these things I found as grateful and comforting as the cocoa you wot of. Yes, the comedy is wholesome.

More wholesome, mind you, than the original. Not that you will find much perilous stuff in this or any other of the plays which fill the ten volumes of Labiche's "Théâtre Complet." But there is one speck, just a little one, on the surface of *Les Petits Oiseaux*, and that Mr. Grundy has delicately rubbed off. You remember the scene in which Mr. Goldfinch learns from his wife that some one has just tried to kiss her. The some one is Uncle Gregory, Goldfinch's brother, who has been lunching a little too freely. In the original the delinquent is Goldfinch's nephew Dick, who is represented from the outset of the play as making serious love to his aunt. Moreover, Labiche makes this youngster get into debt on account of a young girl he has betrayed. There is nothing of this in *A Pair of Spectacles*. *La bête humaine* is not allowed to show his cloven hoof.

Dick is whitewashed, and the play becomes completely deodorised.

Note, too, another improvement of Mr. Grundy's. He has struck a deeper chord than Labiche in the character of Goldfinch. He has sounded the note of seriousness, a note never once heard in the whole repertory of Labiche. It is on record that this author once wrote to a confidant, "Je n'ai jamais pu prendre l'homme au sérieux"—I have never been able to take mankind seriously. His sole aim as a playwright has been laughter. Now one needn't be supersubtle to see that perpetual laughter presupposes an immense disdain. To regard men as unimportant puppets; to study them seriously as you would some queer insect; to set them playing monkey-tricks up and down a string—this is to take a mighty contemptuous view of humanity. It is as good as to declare that humanity is not worth a deeper analysis; that you can't look at it for laughing; that you won't even do it the honour of being afraid of it; that at best it is only good to amuse children, big and little. In this way you get the seeming paradox that Labiche's laughter tends to work towards the wrong side of the mouth—just because he has "never been able to take mankind seriously." Here it is that Mr. Grundy's English instinct does him a good turn. He knows that we, whatever Labiche may do, shall prefer to take Goldfinch seriously. Hence the artful introduction of the Biblical texts; hence Goldfinch's repeated declarations of his faith that wealth is only a trust; hence, one may add, Mr. Hare's frequent transitions from mere eccentric humour to tones of grave conviction. From this point of view I am not quite sure that Mr. Hare's scene of extravagant jealousy, when Goldfinch confronts his wife with what he supposes to be the evidence of an intrigue with the curate, is not an artistic mistake. It gets, I am aware, the loudest laugh of the evening; but it blurs the spectator's impression of the seriousness underlying the character. There is a momentary loss of esteem, and barring that little passage, I do protest that I esteem simple Mr. Benjamin Goldfinch as much as I esteem simple Sir Roger de Coverley.

But now I think of it, we couldn't afford to sacrifice that scene of jealousy, for therein is contained the one opportunity for Miss Kate Rorke. How cleverly she seizes it! Watch her facial play while Mr. Hare is raving at her and brandishing that tell-tale umbrella: the merry pout, the twinkling glance, the slightly-raised eye-brow; surprise and amusement struggling not to become vexation. Note that triumphant exit of hers when Mr. Hare demands the name of the man who has tried to kiss her.

He: His name, madam! His name, I say!

She: Shall I tell you? (*A pause: then with a provoking little toss of the head*) No! Just to punish you! (*Exit, slamming the door as violently as a well-bred lady in a Hampstead villa and a coquettish morning-cap may*.)

Reichenberg could not play this scene with more *finesse*.

AT WESTMINSTER.

(December, 1890.)

CRITICS, under the soporific influence of a matinée performance, have been seen (and, indeed, heard) to turn a playhouse into a dormitory, but the Queen's Scholars of St. Peter's College, Westminster, are probably the only persons to whom it has occurred to turn a dormitory into a playhouse. Interesting as one cannot choose but find the old Westminster play and the young Westminster scholars, one shivers in that *locus pænitentiæ* which serves them for a playhouse; it is something too monkish, too cloistral, for comfort; and Little Dean's Yard itself were perchance less draughty. But to hint this is to be ribald, if not impious. Where else, pray, do you get a prologue recited by a school-captain in black silk knee-breeches? Where else do you see the ladies (they have a little pen to themselves) so plainly taught their place? Where else do you hear the back benches volleying applause with a precision that only birch-rods could enforce? Where else do you find the front benches sanctified by at least one Dean with an order (not of admission, but of the Garter), and a phalanx of Minor Canonry—not to mention the awful vision of the Head Master's gown and bands? These delights, or some of them, strike one as the material embodiment of the school's " rich spiritual inheritance from the past," spoken of this year in the Prologue. Nevertheless, the Westminster play boasts one inheritance from the past, neither spiritual nor rich; in fact, sadly in need of repair. I refer to the scenery, of which a portion was so rotten as to fall, at one of the performances of the *Adelphi* this winter, from its frame to the stage. This accident caused the venerable Micio to skip about in a way not prescribed by the stage-manager, and thus gave to his ensuing half-line,

"Defessus sum ambulando,"

the unexpected force of a "topical" illusion.

You are familiar of course with the plot of the *Adelphi*? "Vous sçavez le latin sans doute?" said the philosopher to M. Jourdain. "Ouÿ," was the reply, "ouÿ, mais faites comme si je ne le sçavois pas." So, although you are familiar with the plot, it will perhaps be well for me to narrate it, all the same. Here it is, in doggrel perpetrated some years ago by an Old Westminster:—

"Two brothers once in Athens dwelt of old,
    Though widely did their dispositions differ;
One loved the country, was a churl and scold,
    The other bland and gentle as a zephyr.

"Demea, the churl, had once a wife—since dead,
    And, as it seems, he did not much regret her;
Micio, the bland, had not been so *miss*-led,
    And never——"

But stay! Let me try (in Mr. Andrew Lang's favourite quotation from the Cookery Book) "another way." Every one, with whom nescience is not a foible, knows the plot of the *Pair of Spectacles* at the Garrick. Now, with just a little "humouring," a little manipulation of the truth (I make the matter-of-fact a present of this admission), it ought not to be difficult to show a practical identity between the plot of Mr. Grundy's (or rather M. Labiche's) play and that of Terence's *Adelphi*. You remove the scene from a villa at Hampstead to a terrace at Athens, with a distant view of the Acropolis. The two brothers, Gregory (from Sheffield) and Benjamin, you will re-name Demea and Micio, the two youngsters becoming Æschinus and Ctesipho. Mrs. Benjamin, of course, will have to disappear: no Roman playwright would have ventured to show you a matron in her own home. For the butler and parlourmaid, you will have to substitute slaves, the faithful Geta and the splendidly mendacious Syrus. These purely formal changes effected, you find your identity established. But take note that it is an inverted identity. In the Garrick play, the scapegrace son borrows the good reputation (you remember, *e.g.*, that little incident of the photograph and the barrister's robes) of the other. In the *Adelphi*, it is the other who takes on his own shoulders the evil reputation of the scapegrace. At the Garrick, the *nodus* of the action is the sudden (and sincere) perversion of the "bland" Micio-Benjamin to the philosophy of the "churl," Demea-Gregory. In the *Adelphi*, it is the equally sudden (and ironic) conversion of the churlish Demea to the blandness of Micio. The attempt to trace this parallel is not, of course, to be construed into an insinuation that M. Eugène Labiche and Mr. Sydney Grundy have consciously plagiarised from Terence.

The performance at Westminster shows, however, that the real interest of the *Adelphi*, for a modern audience, lies not in its plot, but in the purely episodic scenes between the iracund Demea and the impudent Syrus. The passage in which the slave mimics the old martinet to his face, and that in which he sends him all over the city on a fool's errand, would not be out of place in eighteenth-century comedy. Indeed, it is curious to note how many types and features there are in the play which, after the lapse of two thousand years, still retain their hold on the stage. The indulgent and the tyrannical father, the scapegrace son; these, of course, are eternal. Geta, the faithful slave, is the direct ancestor of Shakespeare's Adam, of Nöel in *La Joie fait Peur*, of Jakes in *The Silver King*, and of I know not how many more tedious, limpet-like domestics. As for Sostrata, the ill-used mother-in-law, any contemporary farce will show you to what monstrous proportions that lady has developed on the stage. In Hegio, the "family-friend," is it fanciful to detect a long line of *raisonneurs*, including the Cléantes of Molière, to end in the Thouvenins (and perhaps the Des Ryons?) of Dumas *fils*? Then there is the wily, familiar, obsequious, sapient, lying, drunken slave Syrus—hats off, please, to Syrus!—for Syrus begat Scapin, and Scapin begat Figaro, and Figaro begat—well, among other little matters, the French Revolution, Mr. Punch, and the whole race of critics (including—*mehercle!* as Syrus himself would say—the dramatic).

Aye! Even the latter-day critic is anticipated in the *Adelphi*. When Micio turns upon Demea in Act v. to inquire the reason of his sudden conversion, with the question "*quæ res tam repente mores mutavit tuos?*" do I not hear Mr. Clement Scott asking the very same question of Beau Austin about his proposal of marriage to Dorothy Musgrave, while M. Francisque Sarcey buttonholes Terence to explain to him that "the art of drama is the art of preparations"?

All the Westminster boys spout their Latin with commendable distinctness, but have yet to learn that one of the rudiments of acting is to look at the audience, and not at your toes. J. S. Phillimore's Syrus was the best thing in the cast; and next to that, perhaps, the Geta of C. F. Watherston, a good realisation of Demea's description of the character:—

> "... ut captus est servorum, non malus
> Neque iners ..."

The youngsters found freer scope for their high spirits in the Epilogue, which of course was as usual "palpitating with actuality." Syrus became a police magistrate (in scarlet and ermine) who sentences Ctesipho to *septem dies cum duro labore* for photographing an Irish shindy. Ctesipho, whose Latin was not without an appropriate touch of the brogue, was hurried off by the *Balforiana cohors* while shouting "*Dulcest pro patriâ Gladstonioque mori!*" Æschinus was a Guardsman, exiled to Bermuda; Sannio, a matrimonial agent sued by Sostrata. Needless to say there were allusions to *lympha Koch-ta* and the *Salvans Exercitus*. On the whole, good boyish fooling.

A. W. PINERO.

"LADY BOUNTIFUL."

(*Garrick Theatre, March*, 1891.)

YES; it *is* an obvious remark—which must have occurred in a score of criticisms—that the subject of Mr. Pinero's *Lady Bountiful* suggests a novel rather than a play. One cannot always be ignoring the obvious—paradoxes, like partridges, must have their "close time" now and again—and my criticism will have to be one of the score which Mr. William Archer has foreseen. But I shall take my courage in both hands and venture, for once, to disagree with Mr. Archer when he goes on to contend that the obvious remark ought to imply commendation rather than censure. Certainly, the novel is superior to drama in that it takes a wider, more leisurely, more minute survey of human life. Let us, then, encourage every attempt to transfer to the stage the most advanced methods of fiction. My quarrel with Mr. Pinero is that he does not lay hold of those advanced methods. The sort of novel which his story suggests is the old-fashioned English "chronicle" novel, rambling, diffuse, quasi-biographical, artless, unsymmetrical, wanting in all sense of proportion. Of this sort, to be sure, are the novels of Dickens and Thackeray; but all attempts to transfer the novels of Dickens to the stage have been hideous failures, and any such attempts in the case of Thackeray have been so obviously hopeless as never even to have been ventured upon. Why? For the simple reason that novels of this sort do not give us unity of impression. The modern French novel, with its advanced methods —and it is, of course, the methods of the modern French novel which the French rebels against the well-made play have attempted to transfer to the stage—does give us this unity of impression. A drama which does not give us this unity cannot be said to constitute a play: it is a sequence of different plays; it is not a work of art, one and indivisible. One of the notoriously weak points of the English novel has always been its failure to give us this unity. In this matter, whatever its general superiority, it is inferior to drama. We shall hardly strengthen the English drama by transferring to the stage the peculiar weaknesses of English fiction.

And that, it seems to me, is what Mr. Pinero has done in *Lady Bountiful*. The bare outlines of his story are those of the story of "The Newcomes" (and for that matter of a round dozen of other less famous English novels). I do not speak of the filling-in, the treatment, the atmosphere; these are widely different in book and play; but the two love-plots are practically identical. The hero in both book and play is beloved by two women; marries the wrong one; becomes a widower; and ultimately weds his first love. In the book there is a certain half-hearted attempt to give us unity of impression by reducing Clive's marriage with Rosey to the proportion of an episode, by slurring over the pathos of her death (we are only allowed to read it in *The Times*), and by giving Ethel a character and a story of her own, independent of her relations to Clive. Contrast this with the play. There the marriage of Dennis Heron with Margaret Veale ceases to be an episode. It becomes, for a time, the play itself. For a whole act our attention is concentrated on that marriage; all our sympathies are engaged by it. Our previous interest in the love-affair of Dennis and Camilla Brent is abruptly arrested by it. Camilla merely lags superfluous, while all our tears are demanded for the pathetic figure of Margaret, who is made to die before our eyes. Unity of impression might have been secured by combining the Margaret-subject with the Camilla-subject. The jealousy of Margaret for Camilla might have been developed in a passionate scene between the two women. (Ah! don't ask me how! That would be Mr. Pinero's business, not mine.) Dennis might have been shown as still hankering after his first love, and, perhaps, placed in a sort of Captain Macheath situation. Or (had not Mr. Pinero's avowed intention been to tell "a simple tale to speed a young maid's hour—no lust, not a Commandment broke") the dying Margaret, Dennis's mistress, instead of wife, might have entreated Camilla, his lawful spouse, to adopt the new-born child—as happens in the *Musotte* of M. Guy de Maupassant. By some such means as these we might have had the element of uncertainty, spiritual conflict, the tying and untying of a knot, without which there can be no real drama. And we should have had unity of impression, we should have had a play. What we do get is two plays: one showing the wooing of Camilla by Dennis, their separation, and ultimate union (Act i., first half of Act ii., Act iv.); the other showing the marriage of Dennis with Margaret, their poverty, and Margaret's death (second half of Act ii., Act iii.). The two plays appeal to different sets of interests and sympathies, with the result that the spectator, asked to shift his attention abruptly from the Camilla-subject to the Margaret-subject, and then back again, becomes confused, irritated, and finally languid. And all because the dramatist has attempted to transfer to the stage the (anything but advanced) methods of the (wrong sort of) novel.

A more serious grievance is prompted by the reflection that the author of *Lady Bountiful* is also the author of *The Profligate*. It is simply deplorable that a man of Mr. Pinero's calibre should condescend "to speed a young maid's hour," when he might be tackling serious problems, dramatising the great crises of life, giving fully developed adults something to set their brains at work. In the name of this young maid he fobs us off with a couple of commonplace love-stories. Not being, as it happens, a young maid, I regard this as a flagrant shirking of duty on Mr. Pinero's part towards myself, not to mention some hundreds of thousands of my fellow-playgoers. Really, if our young maids are going to spoil our foremost dramatists for us in this way, the sooner we import that old Minotaur the better. But enough of devil's —and minotaur's—advocacy! With all its shortcomings *Lady Bountiful* is a play which one would be sorry not to have seen, and still more sorry not to have heard. For not only is it admirably put upon the stage—the riding-school of Act ii., the lodging-house basement of Act iii., and the church interior of Act iv., are triumphs of *mise-en-scène*—not only does it abound in ingenious details of stage " business," Mr. Pinero, like Sardou, having that invaluable gift *le doigté du dramaturge*, the fingering of the playwright, but its dialogue is fresh, delicate, direct, and quietly humorous. Note, among the "business" ingenuities, how every detail of the second scene is made to contribute to the general atmosphere of "horseyness," and how the interview between the lovers in the church scene gains in interest by the mere fact that it takes place in total darkness. This "coal-hole" effect, however, is not entirely new to the stage, as some critics have rashly supposed. We had already seen it at the Lyceum, in the last act of *The Lyons Mail*, and something very much like it in the third tableau of that wonderful *Mort du Duc d'Enghien*, which M. Antoine gave us a year or two ago at the Royalty. It matters not that this coal-hole effect was a mere accident. Something, it appears, had gone wrong with the electric light. If so, I can only say it was as lucky an accident as the fall of Newton's apple, and the Garrick stage-manager will be unworthy of any more gifts from the Fairy Good-fortune if he does not arrange for that electric light to go wrong nightly.

"IN CHANCERY."

(Revived November, 1890.)

THE revival of Mr. Pinero's *In Chancery* at Terry's Theatre, while the same writer's *Cabinet Minister* is still in full career at the Court, furnishes a good object-lesson in what, for want of a better term, must be called the science of comparative dramatics. In his Court series of farces Mr. Pinero has worked out a formula of his own—or, rather, has successfully adapted one of the great French master's. This consists in expanding Molière's trick of putting the Gérontes of this world into the sack—

Dans ce sac dont Scapin l'enveloppe—

by showing dignitaries—a dean, a police magistrate, a Secretary of State—in situations the reverse of dignified, whence they are not allowed to escape until, like their prototype, they have been well belaboured by Scapin's *coups de bâ-â-â-ton*.

The initial situation of *In Chancery* takes us much farther back than Molière—as far back, in fact, as the Sophoclean drama. It is that of a man ignorant of his own identity, the consequences of whose ignorance may be deeply tragic or extravagantly ludicrous. Make this man's ignorance proceed from the fact that he is a foundling, let him marry his mother and slay his father, and, hey presto! you have succeeded (provided always that you are a Sophocles) in imagining the *Œdipus Tyrannus*. Now degrade your man from king to commercial traveller, make his ignorance arise from a lesion of the brain caused by a railway accident, deposit him helpless, penniless, memoryless, and (as it turns out) nameless in a wayside inn, and you have the Montague Jolliffe of Mr. Pinero's *In Chancery*. It would be unfair, of course, to scrutinise the parallel too closely. The new Œdipus does not marry his mother, but he does come within an ace of committing bigamy with his landlord's daughter, and only just escapes arrest as the runaway husband of another lady—to such dire purpose has oblivion scattered over him her poppy. If Mr. Pinero complains, as he justly may, that the filiation of his piece to the Sophoclean drama is fanciful, he will at least give me leave to trace its first suggestion to a leading case in mental pathology—the famous case of the soldier in the American Civil War, with a fragment of shell embedded in his skull, whose memory of his past self was an absolute blank until the fragment was removed. A certain order of play-goers will be able to laugh at the extravagancies of farce with an easier conscience when they find them thus placed on a respectable scientific basis.

For laugh at Mr. Pinero's farce all play-goers must, so whimsical is its dialogue, so diverting its intrigue, so droll the helpless embarrassment of its hero as depicted by Mr. Edward Terry. Criticism will not do justice to this comedian until a new notation has been invented. We have a notation for musical sounds, and the old ballet-masters had one for dance-rhythms (see, on this head, the curious choregraphic treatise of one Jehan Tabourot—if you can find it), but where is the notation for the speaking voice? It must be contrived if ever we are to represent on paper the gamut of strange sounds which Mr. Edward Terry traverses in the brief course of a three-act farce. He has been called an "animated clarinet," but that is a wholly inadequate description of a voice which ranges from the squeaks of the piccolo and the ear-piercing fife, through the whole range of the "wood-wind," down to the buzz of the bassoon. The peculiar danger, of course, of such an organ is that it sometimes tempts its possessor to illustrate the old saw of *vox et præterea nihil;* and Mr. Terry has not always resisted this temptation. He did not, for instance, in his penultimate part, that of Dick Phenyl in *Sweet Lavender.* But as Montague Jolliffe he is something more than an oboe in trousers. He presents a natural, unexaggerated, and all the more droll because unexaggerated, picture of the mishaps of a man without a memory. His revival of *In Chancery* will strengthen his reputation, and will not weaken Mr. Pinero's.

ROBERT BUCHANAN.

"CLARISSA."

(Vaudeville Theatre, February, 1890.)

AT the first performance of one of Voltaire's tragedies, freely purloined from a Greek original, it is said that the author leant out of his box and shouted at the somnolent pit, "Applaud, you idiots; that's Sophocles, not Voltaire!" At the Vaudeville I hid behind a fair neighbour's monumental hat, in mortal terror lest the author, leaning out of his box, and catching me falling asleep in the wrong place, should shout, "Don't yawn, you idiot; that's Richardson, not Buchanan!" Which is which? The harassing question recurred with each fresh entry, each successive incident. Is it Buchanan, and may I yawn publicly? Or is it Richardson, and must I dodge behind my neighbour's hat? Into such an abyss of doubt is one cast by respect for a British classic whom one has neglected to read. Neglected is hardly the word; it should be, refused. Despite the injunctions of my pastors and masters; despite the temptation of getting the whole set of eight volumes from a second-hand bookstall for fourpence, I have always refused to read "Clarissa Harlowe." If any one asks why, let him be answered by this scrap of dialogue reported by Boswell:

"ERSKINE: Surely, sir, Richardson is very tedious?
JOHNSON: Why, sir, if you were to read Richardson for the story, your impatience would be so much fretted that you would hang yourself."

Perhaps some rude person, who fails to perceive the true inwardness of Impressionist criticism, will say that he doesn't care a straw whether I have read the book or not, that that is my affair, not his. Let such an objector just consider what would have happened if I *had* read Richardson's book without going to see Buchanan's play. Obviously my judgment would have been cut-and-dried in advance. It would, according to time-honoured practice in such cases, have been a string of lamentations over the shocking fashion in which the audacious modern had mangled the venerable ancient. The word sacrilege would have appeared at least a dozen times in my notice, and there would have been dark allusions to body-snatchers, resurrection men, ghouls and other such fearsome things. Now, my ignorance of the book has saved me from all this.

Moreover, it enabled me at the Vaudeville to enjoy that pleasant sport known to the French code as *la récherche de la paternité*. Where did Richardson come in? Where Buchanan? And where Dumanoir, Guillard, and Clairville? But who, you ask, are Dumanoir, Guillard, and Clairville? Mr. Buchanan himself answers this question in a note on the programme. They were the joint authors of a French dramatisation of Richardson's novel, made famous by the acting of Bressant and Rose Chéri. Mr. Buchanan (or more probably the programme compiler—an accurate programme the eye of man hath not seen) says this play was produced at the Gymnase in 1842. The correct date is August, 1846. Jules Janin and Théophile

Gautier went into ecstasies over this piece; and when a French dramatic critic of 1846 became ecstatic the air was thick with meteoric adjectives, I can tell you. But it is perhaps time that my own adjectives began to coruscate. Let them flash first upon Mr. Thomas Thorne. The first guess I hazard is that there is mighty little Richardson in this gentleman's part. One may get at that *à priori*. A leading character, obviously, must be found for the manager, and the only leading characters in this novel (one may be permitted to know so much without having read the book) are Lovelace and Clarissa. Now, the wildest imagination refuses to conceive Mr. Thomas Thorne as Lovelace, and it is equally difficult to suppose him playing Clarissa. Hence I take the part of Philip Belford to be the joint invention of the English and French dramatists. Belford is a drunken ne'erdoweel, turned misogynist by the death of his wife and the ruin of his only sister, Hetty. Through the man's sottishness glimpses of a better nature are perceived. Hardly has he helped Lovelace in the plot against Clarissa when he repents, and, finding that it is Lovelace who is his sister's betrayer, resolves to save the woman and kill the man. In the first enterprise he fails, for the same drugged wine which makes Clarissa Lovelace's helplesss victim disables Philip Belford just as he is on the point of effecting her rescue. But it is Belford's sword by which Clarissa is avenged. The actor overelaborates the part in his own well-known fashion, though apparently to the complete satisfaction of those play-goers who like their pathos sung—and sung *adagio*—and sung on one note. His quaint humour, which made the fortune of his Partridge and his Parson Adams, here gets no scope. We shall probably be safe in assuming that what Belford *is* belongs to Mr. Buchanan, what he *does* to our friends Dumanoir, Guillard, and Clairville. Hetty Belford, Philip's fallen sister, is, one supposes, Buchanan *du plus pur:* she has that melodramatic air which betrays late nineteenth-century work. One may risk the same guess about Captain Macshane, a Sir Pandarus of Troy, with a broad Scotch accent, who masquerades as a clergyman and makes a happily frustrated attempt to sing "The Gowden Vanitee." It is a droll part, and is "composed" with care by Mr. Fred Thorne. Clarissa's heavy and unrelenting father becomes a terrible personage in the hands of Mr. Harbury. Fortunately he disappears after the first act. So— not so fortunately—does Mr. Solmes, Clarissa's rich elderly suitor, a character very cleverly sketched by Mr. Cyril Maude. Miss Mary Collette plays a little rustic coquette prettily, and Messrs. F. Grove and Frank Gillmore both give the conventional stage picture of an eighteenth-century man of fashion, *i.e.*, satin clothes, many flourishes of the hat, frequent "Fore Gads," and a strut.

Coming to the Lovelace, I find myself in a quandary. You see, my ignorance of Richardson's book prevents me from knowing what sort of a Lovelace Richardson's Lovelace was. Mr. Thalberg may be that man. If he be, why, so much the worse for Lovelace and Richardson and Mr. Thalberg. Whatever may be the case with the printed page (especially in Richardson's epistolary form where there is room for the slow development of a psychological study) one cannot stand a character of this sort, a creature of unqualified moral turpitude, on the stage of to-day (outside sheer melodrama) unless one gets an intellectual impression. I cannot be interested in a mere well-dressed rake. No doubt the Don Juans of real life are often poor, empty creatures. Women have a strange taste. But if you bring Don Juan on the stage, you must make him a Don Juan that satisfies my imagination. There must be a magnificence about the fellow; he must be a virtuoso in the Fine Art of Don Juanism; must have *maestria;* must be a philosopher like the Don Juan of Molière; a heroic figure that will not make Leporello's catalogue sound ridiculous; a host not too puny to invite the statue of the commander to supper. How else will you satisfy a generation that (if it does not read "Clarissa Harlowe") is very familiar with Feuillet's M. de Camors and Daudet's Duc de Mora? I recognize the dramatist's difficulty here. A character of this complexity is not easily rendered by the simple methods of the stage. It is something like the difficulty Lamb complained of in the representation of Shakespeare's colossal villains. They lose their intellectual charm before the footlights, where, *e.g.*, "the profound, the witty, the accomplished Richard" is apt to become a mere ogre. Now, this Lovelace is no virtuoso in Don Juanism. He is no seducer, even. He is a vulgar cheat, who flourishes his handkerchief, takes snuff with an air, uses foul drugs, and—one must put a brutal fact brutally—commits a rape upon his victim. Don't ask me to be interested in this fellow. He is a poor, cheap, sawdust-stuffed creature, an eighteenth-century *vibrion*. And when Belford kills this *vibrion*, as Clarkson in Dumas' play kills the other, the *vibrion's* return to gasp out his dying repentance over his dead victim's body only fills me with disgust. A Don Juan who cannot "see it through" —bah! All this is not to say that Mr. Thalberg fails to do his best with the part provided for him. But if that part be Richardson's Lovelace I shall never regret my ignorance of Richardson. Of Miss Winifred

Emery's Clarissa one can only say that it is, in Mr. Ruskin's pet phrase, "an entirely beautiful" performance. The reading of the poor artless little will in the final scene is tear-compelling. And, while you weep, you enjoy the pleasure of harmless speculation into the bargain. Is this a true Richardson tear? you wonder, as it trickles down your nose. Or is it a Buchanan drop? What if it should be only a spurious French tear, a tear of collaboration, the tear of Dumanoir, Guillard, and Clairville? Here are diverting questions, the answers to which Miss Blanche Amory may write down in that little volume of hers, entitled "Mes Larmes."

J. K. JEROME.

"NEW LAMPS FOR OLD."

(*Terry's Theatre, February*, 1890.)

MR. JEROME calls his farce "A (comparatively speaking) New and Original Play," and says this is done "to clinch the critics," who, it seems, have a bad habit, whenever a new play is produced, of enumerating several old plays which it closely resembles. It is clear that Mr. Jerome (like most playwrights, and, indeed, not a few critics) misconceives the true function of criticism. Serviceable criticism traces the filiation of dramatic ideas, sorts and labels them, and cultivates a keen eye for family-likenesses. Keeping this keen eye wide open, it observes the same *motif* persistently reappearing, under varying forms, throughout the ages. For example, it notes the idea underlying the *Eumenides* of Æschylus cropping up again in *Hamlet* two thousand years later. It finds Electra's recognition of Orestes in the *Choephori* by means of his footprints and lock of hair reappearing as the strawberry-mark on the left arm in an Adelphi melodrama. Naturally, in announcing his discovery, the critic, like the jabberwock, chortles in his joy. It gives him (who, in what Mr. Cyrus Blenkarn calls a blackguard world, gets all the kicks) a momentary sense of superiority to the playwright (who gets all the ha'pence). Surely Mr.

Jerome will not grudge the poor critic a gratification so innocent? Anyhow, I for one am not to be "clinched" by his "comparatively speaking." On the contrary, his defiance only enhances the pleasure with which I tell him that his farce *New Lamps for Old* reminds me very strongly of an old, old play by Marivaux, and a very recent one by Meilhac. Let not Mr. Jerome suppose that I accuse him of plagiarism. Heaven grant that I could! For the delicate marivaudage of Marivaux, the subtlety and elegance of Meilhac, happen to be more to my own taste than the literary graces of a playwright whose hero calls himself a "Juggins," whose heroines exclaim "What the devil!" and whose old men talk of "getting the needle." These little Jeromiads betray a Muse too prone to flirtation with our old friend 'Arry. All that I mean is that Marivaux, Meilhac, and Mr. Jerome K. Jerome have all three been working with one and the same formula.

That formula may be expressed algebraically. A and B love one another, so do C and D. But, for a reason which, being at present undetermined, I will call x, A "carries on" with D, and B with C. Then a general uneasiness (in Act ii.) shows A, B, C, and D that they have made a mistake. There is a resorting in Act iii.; A recognizes that B is his only love, and D rushes into the arms of C.

Now to evaluate our unknown quantity. Firstly, let $x =$ the general perversity and coquettish instinct of woman and the "cussedness" of man. Call A Dorante, and C Damis, B the Comtesse, and D the Marquise. Make them lovers as yet unmarried; give them red heels and *paniers*, powder and patches; supply a Watteau background, with music by Rameau —and you have *L'heureux Stratagème* of Marivaux.

Secondly, let $x=$ the boredom of matrimony and the desire for divorce merely as "a new sensation." This, of course, requires that our lovers shall now have become married couples. Put them in the Paris of the present day; throw in a Brazilian *rastaquouère* —and you have Meilhac's *Pépa*, which Mdlle. Reichenberg and M. Febvre played for us at the Royalty not long ago. Lastly, let $x=$ the desire to throw off the bondage of conventional married life which, in the case of very silly persons, might possibly supervene upon the misreading of Mrs. Mona Caird's theories, and the misunderstanding of Nora's behaviour in Ibsen's *Doll's House*. And note, please, that our third x is very different in kind from the first and second. They were general, applicable to human nature everywhere and at all times; this one is special, it appeals only to the London of to-day, and it implies a satiric intention. Look closely into this x, for there, if anywhere, you will find the novelty and originality of Mr. Jerome's play, in which many prophetic paragraphs have been telling us to expect a burlesque upon what is miscalled Ibsenism. Note, too, that our pairs of lovers are again *ex hypothesi* married couples. A and B (Mr. and Mrs. Honeydew) adore one another, but, after reading Mrs. Mona Caird and seeing *A Doll's House*, each feels it the correct thing to run away from the other. C and D (Postlethwaite and Octavia) have already separated. They only went through the marriage ceremony (as in a famous literary case) to please their friends. Accordingly A elopes with D and B with C. In Act ii. they all meet at the same hotel, and at once find out what a mistake they have made: Mrs. Honeydew is disillusioned about the long-haired poet Postlethwaite when she sees him in carpet slippers and without his wig; the strong-minded and "rationally-dressed" Octavia bores the mild Mr. Honeydew. Just as one couple is on the point of recognizing the other the electric light goes out, and there is a general scramble for the door. In Act iii. you have the return home, every one mud-bespattered and in tatters, after a terrible cross-country experience (inevitable in this kind of farce, see *The Magistrate, Artful Cards*, &c., &c.); then a general reconciliation, resumption of conjugal relations between A and B, C and D—and curtain.

This outline of the plot establishes my point— namely, the identity of Mr. Jerome's formula with that of Marivaux and Meilhac. But, let me add frankly, that it by no means does justice to Mr. Jerome's piece. It leaves out of account, for instance, one of the most amusing personages in the play, one Buster, an old family solicitor, played by Mr. Penley in his best Penleian vein. In spite, once more, of Mr. Jerome's "comparatively speaking," I shall take leave to say that Buster is our old friend Paul Pry (even to the detail of the forgotten umbrella) under a new name; but he is none the less diverting for that. Very diverting, too, are the novel bits of "business" in which the play abounds. There is a lift which, when Buster tumbles into it, immediately starts going up and down, and only allows him time, as he passes and repasses the stage, to interject some screaming absurdity. The sudden extinction of the electric light is another capital detail. It is an "actuality"; it is not without its touch of satire (that should not be lost on one or two club committees one wots of); and it is dramatically effective, for it serves precisely the same purpose of keeping the ball of confusion rolling as the masks in the second act of *Pink Dominos*.

Then again the final fall of the curtain is preceded by a loud bang of the street door, which is a true and ingenious parody of the door-bang in *A Doll's House* —the only true parody, by the way, of the Ibsen play which I can discern in *New Lamps for Old*.

"WOODBARROW FARM."

(Vaudeville Theatre, January, 1891.)

COMING out of the Vaudeville the other night, half pleased, half irritated, by *Woodbarrow Farm*, I confided my doubts and difficulties to a companion. Mr. Jerome's play, you must know, is (to borrow a word invented by Théophile Gautier for some of the theatrical experiments of George Sand) a ruro-drama. Its hero is a young Devonshire farmer, a Country Mouse who becomes—for a time and much to his own discomfort—a Town Mouse. "Why," I asked, "do our dramatists always insist on putting back the clock at least three-score years and ten in their dealings with stage-rusticity? Why is Mr. Jerome's young farmer of to-day, in his dialect, his costume, and his behaviour, an obviously impossible survival of the old stage-coach England? The fag-end-of-the-century farmer, as I find it amusing to conceive him, is a person of supreme elegance, a graduate of an agricultural college, a student, maybe, of Schopenhauer, probably a subscriber to the *Vie Parisienne*, and undistinguishable in dress and deportment (except, perhaps, by his more Grandisonian manner) from a City stockbroker or a Harley Street doctor. I want to see this man on the stage. But I do not ask too much. At a pinch, the farmer of middle-Victorian literature would suffice me, the farmer of George Eliot, George Meredith, or Thomas Hardy. This man has not yet been shown on the stage ; and him, too, I would be content to see. But the actual stage-farmer, the lout who always talks broad Lancashire (in Devon), who always wears velveteens and gaiters, who always scoops up the gravy with his knife—why is this absurd creature still palmed off on play-goers as the real article?" My companion's answer was short and solemn: "It is one of the immutable conventions of the theatre."

Immutable? Let us distinguish. There are two obviously distinct sets of stage-conventions. (1) Conventions which arise from the material conditions of the stage itself ; conditions of space and time. Events which happen in many different places and over a period of years have to happen in one and the same place, and within, at the most, a period of three hours. No one objects to those conventions ; for abolish them and you abolish the theatre along with them. Thus, in *Woodbarrow Farm*, our young farmer is seen at one moment in St. James's Street, and, five minutes later, in his farm on Exmoor. No one is surprised, for this is one of those conventions of dramatic *action* which are immutable. (2) There are conventions which spring from the fact that a play is something which has to be played, and that not before a handful of literary "mandarins," but a mixed audience of average men and women. These conventions represent the dramatist's concessions to the supposed mental and moral limitations of the average crowd ; and their name is legion. *E.g.*, a play must be moral, because a crowd (an aggregate of individuals each under the eye of his neighbours) is always moral ; it must be optimistic, because no crowd is pessimistic ; it must not be constructed on "art for art's sake" principles, because a crowd is not artistic ; its history must be picture-book history ("Louis XI. always kneeling before the images in his hat; Marie Stuart always in tears; Richelieu always cunning"—as Flaubert says), because that is the only history of the crowd—and so on. These, observe, are all conventions of dramatic *characterisation*. It is these which are the real cause of the inferiority of the stage, which always relegate it to the position of "wooden spoon" in the Tripos of the Arts. But they are not immutable. For the crowd changes. It is the dramatists who refuse to change. They regard their audience as composed of Rip van Winkles, or as the petrified courtiers in the Palace of the Sleeping Beauty, and they serve up to the crowd of to-day the conventions demanded by the crowd of fifty years ago.

That Mr. Jerome should have shared this strange delusion of his class is enough to make one rub one's eyes with amazement. For Mr. Jerome is the author of "Stage-Land," one of the most scathing satires on stage-conventions ever written. It seems unkind to condemn Mr. Jerome out of his own mouth; but there is no help for it, for in his book he has supplied us in advance with the severest criticism on his own play. I take up "Stage-Land," and under the heading, "The Adventuress" I read :—

"She sits on a table, and smokes a cigarette. A cigarette on the stage is always the badge of infamy. She seems a smart business woman, and she would probably get on very well if it were not for her friends and relations. They never leave her, never does she get a day or an hour off from them. Wherever she goes, there the whole tribe goes with her. They all go with her in a body when she goes to see her young man, and it is as much as she can do to persuade them to go into the next room, even for five minutes, and give her a chance. . . . She is fond of married life is the adventuress, and she goes in for it pretty extensively. . . . She dresses magnificently," &c., &c.

I turn to *Woodbarrow Farm* and find this description realised to the letter—or rather to the cigarette, the table, the tribe of friends, the husbands, and the dresses. Again, I find in the book:—

"As for the young man who is coming home to see his girl, you simply *can't* kill him. He gets stabbed, and shot, and thrown over precipices, and, bless you, it does him good—it is like a tonic to him. He is for ever being *reported* as dead, but it always turns out to be another fellow who was like him, or who had on his (the young man's) hat. *He* is bound to be out of it, whoever else may be in."

Substitute "claim his estate" for "see his girl," and once more you get Mr. Jerome, on Mr. Squeers's principles, after spelling "w-i-n-d-e-r" in the book, "going and cleaning it" in the play. The invulnerable young man, the stabbing, the shooting, the precipice, the false reports, the other fellow who was like him—all are there. Just one more collation. "Stage-Land" says:—

"The hero has his own way of making love. He always does it from behind. The girl turns away from him, and he breathes his attachment down her back."

Exactly what happens in the wooing of the adventuress by the farmer-hero in *Woodbarrow Farm*. But the book omits one curious detail of stage-courtship. Your conventional hero induces the heroine to suppose that he is wooing her, when all the time he is merely rhapsodising over the charms of another lady—the adventuress, of course. This omission the play is careful to supply.

Yet below these "lowest deeps" of convention, Mr. Jerome can find for us "a lower deep." Before railways were, play-goers liked to have the stage-rustic widely differentiated from the stage-cockney. For him the country was God-made, idyllic; the town, man-made and vicious. The good folk of Devon were as unlike Londoners as though they inhabited another planet. Mr. Jerome, ignoring the "Flying Dutchman," copies the old picture, and gives it to us for the truth of to-day. Upwards of two centuries ago Molière showed us the elephantine gambols of a vulgar, loutish M. Jourdain, trying to learn gentility from dancing-masters and valets. Mr. Jerome (not exactly a Molière, and writing some little time after 1660) puts *his* loutish hero through precisely the same paces. All this because Mr. Jerome, like his fellow-playwrights and my solemn friend, suffers from the *idée fixe* that the conventions of the stage are immutable. Or has Mr. Jerome produced his play as an object-lesson in the faults satirised by his book, so constituting himself his own Sparton Helot? If so, the joke is a dangerous one. Or, perhaps, after all, Mr. Jerome expects us to accept *Woodbarrow Farm* in all good faith on the principle of the credulous Oriental who, when it was suggested to him that the "Arabian Nights' Entertainments" were not exactly gospel-truth, asked—"Why should a man sit down and write so many lies?"

ARTIFICIAL COMEDY.

"OLD SHERRY."

WITH the single and obvious exception of Shakespeare, there is no English dramatist about whom so much nonsense, neither true nor well invented, has been written as about Sheridan. He has had his perfunctory and inadequate biographer in Moore; his maliciously hostile biographer in the egregious Dr. Watkins; his garbage-raking biographer in his son's tutor, Professor Smyth; his slipshod biographer in Mr. Percy Fitzgerald; his ladylike biographer in Mrs. Oliphant: and it has been reserved for Mr. Lloyd Sanders ("Great Writers'" series: Walter Scott, London, 1891), to give us a truthful, intelligible account of what the man did and what the man was.

It is easy to see why Sheridan has hitherto been so maltreated by the bookmakers. To the burgess mind the Sheridanian *ethos* is simply incomprehensible; and when a biographer does not understand, his unvarying resource is to invent. It is the licence of conjecture—"Sheridan, no doubt, must have felt," &c.; "We can imagine with what feelings a man like Sheridan must have received," &c.—which makes the average theatrical biographer the best loathed of his kind. The scapegrace son of an eccentric father and grandson of a *grandpère prodigue*, Sheridan eloped with a public singer, wrote three good plays, mismanaged a great theatre, made a couple of great parliamentary speeches, drank a great deal too much claret and brandy, treated two good wives uncommonly ill, put his trust in a prince, was ruined, and died a broken, starving man: that is the outline of the story Mr. Sanders has to tell, and he tells it well. He nothing extenuates. Take, for instance, the charges of plagiarism. He astutely admits them all—(there are enough of them, goodness knows!)—and then makes the true answer, which in effect is, that their very number is their best refutation. "Strange it is that Sheridan's critics should have failed to see that the very fact Joseph Surface can be traced to so many sources proves that he can owe very little to any of them." From the morality of plagiarism to the morality of what is (or is not, as the case may be) plagiarised is a natural transition. Mr. Sanders points out (after Lamb) that *The School for Scandal* is neither moral nor immoral, but simply non-moral; and he rightly connects this non-morality with the general artificiality of the Sheridanian theatre. But it may be doubted if he perceives the full extent of this artificiality, and he certainly does not explain, as he might profitably have explained, how and why it existed. For instance, he says of *The Rivals:* "Even in the artificial world to which he confined himself, the world of the footlights, Sheridan in this play not unfrequently outrages probability; Bob Acres and Mrs. Malaprop are deliberate caricatures. The lady's verbal misapplications, especially, are too elaborate and too constant for art. Her more ornate flights of blundering are so elaborately ingenious that they are evidently not the natural utterances of the character but the conscious efforts of the dramatist," &c. That is what comes of living in a realistic age. This application of the realistic test, if not itself a Malapropism, is decidedly *mal à propos*. Does Mr. Sanders suppose that Dogberry, Lord Foppington, Mr. Croaker, Lord Ogleby, are not "deliberate caricatures"? Has it not occurred to him that Polonius's advice to Laertes, Jaques's Seven-Ages speech, Hamlet's "To be or not to be," the tirades of Mascarille, are "evidently not the natural utterances of the character but the conscious efforts of the dramatist"? The truth is, he has fallen into the common, almost universal, mistake of ignoring the fundamental difference between the modern theatre and that of which the Sheridanian drama was well-nigh the last noteworthy product. His underlying and altogether erroneous assumption is that the drama was then, as now, *semper et ubique*, an excuse for attempting imitative art: that its main object was to create a perfect illusion. Whereas the drama from its first beginnings up to (and for some years after) Sheridan was an art rather of presentation than of representation; and it was, as it is not now, an art of rhetoric. Material conditions — *e.g.*, lack of the mechanical appliances necessary to produce illusion, defective archæology, the presence of spectators on the stage (whence they were banished not very long before Sheridan wrote), had much to do with this result. So, too, had the demands of a public for which the stage was not only stage but novel, pamphlet, and lecture-platform into the bargain. This theatre was far more unlike ours than its historians are inclined to suspect. It had its own system of histrionics—acting being thus not so much "miming" as "speech-making" or "costume recitation," and the speeches (*cf.* Elia's famous essay) being addressed by the players quite as much to the audience as to one another. And it had its own system of characterisation to suit such histrionics: a system which (in comedy—its effects in tragedy are not here our concern)—demanded brilliant talk from all the *dramatis personæ*, from Fag quite as appropriately as from Captain Absolute, inasmuch as brilliant talk was the principal thing. Of course this resulted in what were "evidently not the natural utterances of the character"; but the "natural" test was never applied, for the simple reason that the drama was not then held to be a reproduction of Nature.

"SHE STOOPS TO CONQUER."

(Criterion Theatre, May, 1890.)

"IT will be said that the theatre is formed to amuse mankind, and that it matters little, if this end be answered, by what means it is obtained. If pieces are denied the name of comedies, yet call them by any other name, and if they are delightful, they are good. Their success, it will be said, is a mark of their merit, and it is only abridging our happiness to deny us an inlet to amusement."

Mr. Wyndham, at least, will not object to my quoting the foregoing words, seeing that they were written by his collaborator in his new piece, Mr. Goldsmith. Yes, assuredly, it *will* be said by apologists for the cavalier treatment Goldsmith's play has received at the Criterion. The apologists will find in the unstinted applause of the audience a full certificate of indemnity for Mr. Wyndham. Mankind — Criterion mankind — was amused. Call the piece farce instead of comedy; yet, as it delighted, it remains good. Mr. Wyndham knows his public. He knows that they care very much for Charles Wyndham, and nothing at all for the inviolability of classic texts. He knows that it would be only "abridging their happiness" to deny them the "inlet to amusement" afforded by an outlet of unscrupulous gag.

All this will be said. Yet I shall take leave to answer it with another quotation from Mr. Wyndham's collaborator, with Mr. Burchell's "Fudge!" My happiness is abridged, though the Criterion public cheer never so wildly. I admire Mr. Charles Wyndham as well as they, but

> I could not love thee, Charles, so much,
> Loved I not Goldsmith more.

None could play Goldsmith better than Mr. Wyndham, if he would but treat Goldsmith's lighter moods a little less in the spirit of Palais-Royal farce, and his heavier moods with a little less of the hysteric fervour of *David Garrick*. But if he could not give us the spirit of Goldsmith, at least he might have left us the letter. I do not complain of his cutting down the five acts of *She Stoops to Conquer* into three. The rule in these matters is as plain as a pikestaff. You may leave out as much as you please of a classic text, on the condition that you add nothing of your own. Sins of omission here are venial; it is the sins of commission that are damnable, and these, at the Criterion are legion. Out of the legion I content myself with taking three, italicising the interpolations.

> HASTINGS (to MARLOW): Cicero never spoke better.
> MARLOW: *Didn't he? Then I'm sorry for Cicero!*

Again, when Hastings tells Mrs. Hardcastle that fifty is the fashionable age in town.

> Mrs. HARD.: Seriously? Then I shall be too young for the fashion.
> HAST.: *Oh, no, Madam!* (*confused*) *I mean —Oh, yes, Madam!*

Again, in the garden scene, as Mrs. Hardcastle hides from the supposed highwayman.

> TONY: When I cough be sure to keep close. *Climb up a tree, mother.*
> Mrs. HARD.: *Oh, Tony, I've fallen into a ditch!*

The substitutions are almost as numerous as the interpolations. All the spades become agricultural implements. "Lie" becomes "fib," "belly-full" becomes "stomach-full," and Mrs. Hardcastle (in Hastings' letter) is no longer called a "hag" but a "hen," in order that a favourite low comedian may begin to cluck-cluck. In fine, the play is a new play, a rattling Criterion farce, not perhaps a bad thing in its way; but, with no wish to depreciate that way, one may be minded to say, *comme dit l'autre*, "The old is better." The general protest against playing old comedy in the "modern spirit," has elicited an amusing counter-protest from Mr. Wyndham. "How," he asks, "is one to cast the mantle of antiquity over the antics of Tony Lumpkin? How am I to laugh without a nineteenth-century ring in the voice; or by what alchemy can I stay the trickling of the anachronistic tear?" How, he goes on, is he "to antedate a tear, a laugh, or a sigh?" All this is only Mr. Wyndham's witty way of saying that, being a modern man, he must needs, willy-nilly, act always in a modern spirit. So stated, the argument is at once seen to prove too much. Must a modern actor play Othello or Coriolanus in a modern spirit? Must a modern Hamlet perforce deliver his address to the players in the familiar tone of some contemporary stage-manager? Must a modern Lady Macbeth, when she dismisses her guests with "A kind good night to all," do it in a nineteenth-century Mayfair tone, as who should say, "And thank you all *so* much for a quite *too* charming evening"? When Mr. Edwin Booth, as the Noble Dane, observed to Ophelia that a great man's memory might "outlive his life *haff a yeer*," he was playing in the modern spirit. Was that right? Mr. Wyndham would apparently argue that it was not only right, but inevitable. This *reductio ad absurdum* shows then, I submit to Mr. Wyndham, that the phrase, " playing an old play in too modern a spirit," is not, as he supposes, meaningless.

It is to the desire to obviate this very risk of playing old plays in too modern a spirit that we owe the existence of what are known as stage "traditions." For this Conservatoires and the Théâtre Français exist, and our old Patent Theatres once existed. These institutions are, or were, all so many bulwarks against the " modern spirit." Has Mr. Wyndham perchance ever amused himself by comparing M. Coquelin's Mascarille with the Mascarille of some average French actor in a scratch provincial company? If he has, it must have been clear to him that, over and above the difference between the talents of the actors, there is an element in the one performance altogether lacking in the other. That element is the outcome of the Français " traditions "; it exists because M. Coquelin has learned *not* to play Mascarille in the modern spirit. How, then, is a modern actor *not* to play *She Stoops to Conquer* in " too modern a spirit " ?

The first and foremost rule one can lay down with confidence. He must not modernise the text by the interpolation of nineteenth-century "gag." He must say exactly what Goldsmith intended him to say, and no more. This obvious rule is flagrantly disregarded at the Criterion. I have already given examples of the interpolations. When Young Marlow, in reply to Hastings' "Cicero never spoke better," is made to ejaculate, "Didn't he? Then I'm sorry for Cicero!" he has been pitchforked right out of the eighteenth into the later nineteenth century; he is playing "in too modern a spirit." And interpolated pantomime may be as modern as interpolated speech. In the scene of Marlow's embarrassment, on his introduction to Miss Hardcastle, Mr. Wyndham administers several surreptitious but vigorous kicks to Hastings, by way of signal. Bob Sackett might have done this, but surely not Young Marlow.

The second rule one approaches with more diffidence—not because it is less imperative, but because it is less easy to explain. Put briefly, it is that Goldsmith's play must be rendered in the style of Goldsmith's own players. What was that style? It was a style appropriate to the age—a highly artificial age, remember, an age of strongly-marked "manner" and richly-coloured "character," an age of elegances, conventions, formalities, ceremonies, all incompatible with the railroad speed of modern life. Acting was then primarily regarded as a declamatory rather than an imitative art. In the playhouse of Goldsmith's day, the modern notion of so-called "natural" acting was not so much as dreamt of. What the actor chiefly aimed at was an effective, somewhat orotund, delivery of the text, and he supplemented this with a studious attention to what Mr. Turveydrop called "deportment." He cared nothing for illusion: he never pretended that he was not *acting*. Hence a certain high-bred artificiality of manner in comedy. Mr. Matthew Arnold would have said it was "in the grand style." Hazlitt called it "gusto." Mr. Stevenson, more greatly daring, would say "gust." The thing has now vanished from our life, and is therefore more difficult than ever to reproduce on the stage. As early as 1820 Lamb complained (see Elia's essay on " Some of the Old Actors ") that it had well-nigh disappeared.

It is difficult, I say, to reproduce the vanished graces of this artificial style on the modern stage; yet the thing must be attempted in any adequate revival of Goldsmith's plays. I think I hear Mr. Wyndham interrupting: "Pray, Mr. Critic, tell us how you would do it." Well, I think if I were stage-managing *She Stoops to Conquer*, I should begin by begging my actors to unlearn nearly all that they had learnt in modern "touch-and-go" farce. I would say to them, "Remember this is not a go-as-you-please competition. Nor is it the Caucus Race in 'Alice in Wonderland.' Nor is rapid pace the thing to drive at. Don't trouble about being 'natural.' Make all your points deliberately. 'Underline' as much as possible. Don't be afraid of over-emphasis. Above all don't act with 'conviction.' Wear your characters 'lightly, like a feather.' Take your audience into your confidence. No nonsense about realism; no talking up stage, or with your back turned; come right down to the footlights and spout over them. In short, do most of the things that, in modern plays, you rightly avoid. You are playing an artificial play, written for an artificial age. Be, then, yourselves artificial." Something of this sort, I think, Mr. Wyndham has said to himself in planning the capital scene of the play, that of Marlow's first interview with Miss Hardcastle. Many play-goers have found fault with this scene on the very ground on which, I confess, it strikes me as admirable. Mr. Wyndham, they say, is only pretending to be shy; he is obviously acting. I am perverse enough to believe that this is

"SHE STOOPS TO CONQUER." 183

just the artificial manner Lee Lewis and his immediate successors in the part adopted. Unfortunately, Mr. Wyndham does not sustain the artifice to the end. In the last scene with Miss Hardcastle—("By heaven! she weeps. This is the first mark of tenderness I ever had from a modest woman," &c.)—he deviates into the sincerity of the modern stage. His voice vibrates with passion. Miss Mary Moore's quavers with suppressed emotion. The pair execute a sort of hysterical love-duet, as though they were giving the last act of *David Garrick*, and the play becomes the very thing which it was professedly written to satirise, a sentimental comedy. The audience know not whether to laugh or to shed what Mr. Wyndham calls "the anachronistic tear." Mr. Wyndham asks (in a queer metaphor) by what alchemy he is to stay its trickling. The answer I would suggest is only apparently paradoxical. Be a little insincere in your sincerity: give up taking the scene *au tragique*.

The second point raised by Mr. Wyndham in his good-humoured expostulation with his critics can be briefly disposed of. It has been generally objected that Goldsmith's comedy is played at the Criterion as a farce. In reply the manager trots out an imposing array of authorities—Dr. Johnson, the elder Colman, Mrs. Inchbald, Horace Walpole, and their tribe—to show that the play was regarded as a farce, and nothing else, from the outset. Obviously, what these respectable fogeys meant was that the *donnée* of the piece, the postulate which it assumes, and the development of the plot, belong to farce. But if the plot of the play—the mistaking of a country-house for an inn and the blunders that ensue—be farcical, assuredly the *treatment* is not. Old Hardcastle is a character-study, so is his wife, so are Young Marlow and Tony Lumpkin character-studies; the scenes between the old man and his guests, between Tony and his mother, between Marlow and Miss Hardcastle are genuine comedy. Now, at the Criterion the treatment—thanks to the general gravitation of a *Pink Domino* management towards "too modern a spirit"—becomes farcical.

"LONDON ASSURANCE."

(Criterion Theatre, December, 1890.)

IN a letter to Monckton Milnes, who had found his patience overtaxed by some of the nicknames too freely bestowed on him by his friends, Sydney Smith writes: "The names of 'Cool of the Evening,' 'London Assurance,' and 'In-I-go Jones,' are, I give you my word, not mine." This was in 1842, and the choice of one at least of the nicknames attests the vogue of a comedy which had been produced at Covent Garden in the previous year—*London Assurance*—by a youngster of nineteen who afterwards called himself Dion Boucicault. In the ensuing half-century the popularity of the piece has slowly dwindled, but never quite to vanishing point. Its vitality, persistent if feeble, has puzzled observers who do not allow for the peculiar conditions of the stage. It is not a classic, say these. It is not literature. It is not life.

The truth is that *London Assurance*, though it has no pretensions to being an organic whole or to holding the mirror up to nature, belongs to a class of plays which the players themselves, despite the indifference of play-goers, will not willingly let die. It is what is known as an actors' play—in this connection the word might perhaps be more correctly written display—a medium, that is, for the exercise of virtuosity—an affair of *bravura* passages, wherein the technical execution is everything and the subject-matter nothing, or next to nothing. Such plays may be taken as the actors' refutation of Euclid, for their aim is to show that a "point" has magnitude, and that a "part" is sometimes greater than the whole. Assuredly it is so with *London Assurance*, in regard to which play the wise man may ask the question, How will Lady Gay Spanker deliver the "Steeple-chase speech?" or how will the "business" between Cool and Meddle be managed? but will at once perceive that to pursue his inquiries into the naturalness of this or that personage, into the credibility of the play as a whole, would be sheer waste of time.

That is the conventional critical standpoint on the subject—and, having adopted it, I feel instantly tempted to shift my ground. Is the play so very unreal as a picture of a time, are its characters so very artificial after all? Might not diligent search reveal some of M. Zola's "human documents" even in this "actors' play"? Suppose, *par impossibile*, that all record and memory of the year 1841 were obliterated except this comedy of *London Assurance*, and let us examine how far it will enable us to "reconstitute an epoch." To begin with, it is evident from the very first scene that in the year of grace—or of the want of it—1841, the social institution known as Tom-and-Jerryism was still flourishing. Charles Courtly "comes home with the milk" in a state of riotous intoxication, and empties his pocket of the knockers which he has wrenched from his neighbours' doors. He is empty-headed, he is vicious, he is, if not a Yahoo, a good deal of a Mohock. Yet the author evidently puts him forward as what would now be called a "sympathetic" personage. For he has everything his own way, is reproved by nobody, and is rewarded in the end with the hand of the pretty girl of the piece.

Here, then, we get our first "document." We have "constated" the existence of Tom-and Jerryism so late as 1841. Picking our way through the dialogue, we find much valuable evidence as to the social habits of the time. Burgundy might then be drunk in the morning. "Come into my room," says Courtly to Dazzle at the breakfast-hour, "and I'll astonish you with some Burgundy." And in the evening it might be followed by brandy-punch. "It was all that cursed brandy-punch on the top of Burgundy," groans Dolly Spanker. Madeira, too, was still in fashion. Dazzle *loq.* : "Max, that Madeira is worth its weight in gold; I hope you have more of it." Max : "A pipe, I think," etc. Smoking-rooms had not yet been established; when the gentlemen wish to practise the vice of cigar smoking, they retire to the billiard-room. For it is still a vice in 1841. "No cigar smoking," says Sir Harcourt ; " Faints at the smell of one," adds Cool— both speaking of a grown man. After dinner, when the ladies have departed, the gentlemen are expected to sing songs. Stage direction : ("Spanker *is heard to sing* ' A Southerly Wind and a Cloudy Sky '— *after verse, chorus* "). Antimacassars justified their existence in 1841. Max Harkaway refers to Sir Harcourt's "oily perfumed locks." From Charles's description of the delights of London to the rustic Grace, we find that the fashionable entertainment was not the opera, but the ballet. The fopperies of Sir Harcourt show that in 1841 we are still in the Age of the Dandies, further evidence of which is forthcoming in Grace's allusion to "our literary dandyisms and dandy literature." In other words, scratch this play and you find both D'Orsay and Bulwer. The entry of Mr. Solomon Isaacs in the last act shows that people were still arrested for debt. And they still travelled from London to Gloucestershire in post-chaises (hence a sharp dis' tinction between the Town Mice and the Country Mice of the play, which gives another "note" of 1841). Duelling (but here our "document" perhaps becomes untrustworthy) did not yet involve a trip across the Channel. Sir Harcourt and Spanker manage their little affair in the billiard-room. Minor points are: that "buttonholing" was not yet a mere figure of speech ("He would actually," says Lawyer Meddle, "have taken the Reverend Mr. Spout by the button"); and that architectural taste was still barbaric ("the fine Elizabethan mansion" of scene 2 has "large French windows at the back ").

So much for *London Assurance* as a "document." And that is not all. Even the language of the play, untrue as it must have been to the actual life, yet reflected a side of the literary taste, of the time. Certainly no living young lady of 1841 ever rhapsodised as Grace Harkaway does:—

"I love to watch the first tear that glistens in the opening eye of morning, the silent song that flowers breathe, the thrilling choir of the woodland minstrels, to which the modest brook trickles applause; these, swelling out the sweetest chord of sweet creation's matins, seem to pour some soft and merry tale into the daylight's ear, as if the waking world had dreamed a happy thing, and now smiled o'er the telling of it."

But read the English of the "Keepsake" and the "Beauty's Annuals." (And, inasmuch as Grace's uncle describes the glories of "the chase in full cry" in precisely the same dithyrambic strain, take note that, long before Ibsen wrote *Ghosts*, "the drama of heredity," the stage had glimpses of the drama of consanguinity.) Even Lady Gay Spanker's amazing "impression" of the hunt :—

"Time then appears as young as love, and plumes as swift a wing. Then I love the world, myself, and every living thing—a jocund soul cries out for very glee, as it could wish that creation had but one mouth that I might kiss it "—

has its historic justification. For Lady Gay was first played by Mrs. Nisbett, and had not Mrs. Nisbett previously achieved fame for her delivery of Constance's glowing description of the raptures of the hunting-field in Sheridan Knowles's *Love Chase?* He, then, who laughs at Dion Boucicault is laughing, all unaware, at Sheridan Knowles.

My excuse for dwelling on the documentary aspect of the play is that Mr. Charles Wyndham, in the present revival at the Criterion, has frankly presented *London Assurance* as a document. For the first time in the history of its revivals, we have its players habited, with punctilious correctness, in the high-collared, wasp-waisted, tight-legged garments of 1841, so that the student of costume may find in every curly wig, stock, *jabot*, military cloak, white beaver hat, turnover shirt-cuff, and satin waistcoat, a documentary ecstasy.

THE OLD MELODRAMA.

"BELPHEGOR."

(*Olympic Theatre, May,* 1891.)

PEOPLE speak too glibly of the illusions of the theatre. It is really the great home of disillusion. A certain play was produced a year or two before you were born, and, therefore, in that particular epoch of the world's history which must always have for you a peculiar fascination. That the world should have got on so well without you just then provokes in you a justifiable resentment. To be sure, the world existed even before the year or two in question. But that was a long time ago—so long that you can disengage your own personality, and regard the matter coldly, as a mere row of figures with ever so many noughts in a scientific encyclopædia. It is the spectacle of the great mundane movement remorselessly going on so close upon your advent which hurts you. That, you feel, as M. Prudhomme felt about the immensity of the ocean, *frise l'impertinence*. To the plays and the players of that particular epoch you can never be indifferent. The thought that the great So-and-so should have chosen to create his famous part of Thingamy just then is galling. He might have waited till you came. But he did not—so you cannot choose but admire him as splendidly audacious. You think more of So-and-so than of Kean or Betterton, and you haunt the slums for little penny-plain-and-twopence-coloured sketches of Thingamy. The years pass, and one day the sight of a theatrical announcement sets your pulse leaping. Thingamy is to be revived—not by So-and-so, for So-and-so is dead and worms have eaten him, but by Whatshisname, who is very much alive and flamboyant on all the posters. You go to see Whatshisname in Thingamy— and you come away disillusioned. You have discovered that there are plays, especially plays dating from that strange, impertinent period immediately preceding your birth, which it is better to read about than to see. You turn sadly to your Ecclesiasticus. "Whoso regardeth dreams is like him that catcheth at a shadow, and followeth after the wind."

These many years have I been dreaming about *Belphegor*. A whole literature of panegyric has grown up around the play and its famous players. When the French original, *Paillasse*, by MM. Dennery and Fournier, was produced at the Gaité in 1850, Théophile Gautier and Jules Janin went into raptures over the playing of its mountebank-hero by Frédéric Lemaître. The profound impression created by Charles Dillon's Belphegor at the Lyceum in 1856 is attested by critics so trustworthy as Dr. Westland Marston and Professor Henry Morley. One of the liveliest pages in Mr. Joseph Jefferson's Autobiography relates how Fechter played the part—off the stage, a mere *impromptu* affair—to two of his fellow actors, and moved them to tears. All this had set me dreaming. There were trailing clouds of glory about my fancied *Belphegor*.

More than that, there seemed to be a real philosophic import in the play. It corresponded to two successive mental states in the unsophisticated playgoer. A child at the play thinks (at least I know one who did think—about the diabolically wise child of to-day I do not venture to speak) that the clown is always a clown, wears his motley and cuts his capers in private life. A year or two later, and the young play-goer becomes aware of the difference between the clown and the man; the contrast between the professional grin and the possibly aching heart interests him. To one of these stages of intelligence *Belphegor* appeals in the character of Flip-Flap, the clown who never ceases from clowning, who balances on his nose the plates which are intended for his own dinner. Flip-Flap is the child's hero. To the other stage the play appeals in the character of Belphegor, the mountebank who has to ply his jokes while his heart is breaking by the desertion of his wife and the starvation of his children. Belphegor is the youth's hero. Here was a play to dream about!

But Mr. Wilson Barrett has robbed me of my dream. He has revived the play, re-written it, and re-named it (quite wrongly, for Paillasse, so called from his suit of blue-and-white check—like the cover of a mattress—was the *pitre*, the Mr. Merryman, of the show) *The Acrobat*. Can this be the piece which delighted Gautier and Janin and our fathers that begat us—this absurd farrago of bombast and pathos? For me there is not one laugh in it, nor one tear. Whose is the fault? Mine, or the Zeit-Geist's, or Mr. Wilson Barrett's? A little, perhaps, the fault of all three. Anyhow, my dream has gone: not poppy, nor mandragora, shall restore it to me; nor Mr. Barrett's masked ball, with its limelit Watteau ballet; nor Miss Winifred Emery's "palely loitering" Madeline; nor the lurid villainy of Mr. Cooper Cliffe's Lavarennes, "assuming the name of the Chevalier de Rollac."

"FORMOSA."

(Drury Lane Theatre, May, 1891.)

AT Drury Lane the other evening my attention was frequently diverted from the performance of *Formosa* on the stage by the performance of a fair neighbour in the stalls. Fair she was in the conventional sense only, for she was of homely features, straight-waisted, and angular; but there was an engaging frankness in her clear blue eyes as she asked me "to loan her a lead-pencil," and a delectable air of business about the way in which she steadily fell to blackening several sheets of paper with the loan. But even a business-like maiden is at the mercy of a tailor-made pocket; and when my neighbour left the theatre at the end of the play, I found her MS. at my feet. My first impulse, as a man, was to post it to the address it contained, but a journalist has no right to be merely human. For him the first rule of conduct is—when you see a piece of "copy," steal it. For my own part, I can never understand why the little huckster who stole his brooms ready-made was not included among Mr. Smiles's "Self-Help" heroes. Besides, the maiden forgot to return my lead-pencil. I have, therefore, determined to print her MS. :—

FROM MISS MIRANDA HOPE, IN LONDON, TO MRS. ABRAHAM C. HOPE, AT BANGOR, MAINE.

May 26th, 1891.

MY DEAR MOTHER,—I was real mad, when I landed on this side, to find I had just missed the Boat

Race. Ever since William Platt took me to see that lovely Greek play at Harvard, I have been right-down curious to see the English collegians. You remember William D. Howells says they are like young Greek gods. Well, it was a real providence that made the manager of Drury Lane—which is called here in the advertisements the National Theater—think of reviving *Formosa*, because that play is all about the Boat Race and Oxford College, and the young Greek gods who belong out there. So I felt like just having to see it. Dear mother, I do *admire* to come to the National Theater. Garrick and Mrs. Sarah Siddons and William C. Macready all played here. They don't play here now—of course, you remember, they are dead; but their names are fixed up all round, and make a lovely show. I feel I am getting European culture here. And that lecturer at the Bangor Museum last fall who said that the English had not found Art was all wrong. Why they are just crowded with it ! They have made the head of their National Theater, Augustus G. Harris, sheriff, because of his services to Art ! But I must tell you about the play. They have called it *Formosa*, because, in Latin, that means real *lovely*. The young men from Oxford College came on in the first scene. They are not fixed up like the young Greek gods in the plaster casts at the Bangor Museum. They wear blue flannel vests and nice clean white pants, and one of them is played by a girl ! My ! It is real interesting to see how they always wear these blue vests and clean white pants, in the rooms of their tutors (whom they call, with boyish familiarity, "dear old dons") and in the saloons of the British aristocracy. All the others, the common people who do not belong to the boat's crew, wear evening dress, if males; and diamonds, if females. And they have a prize-fighter on the stage, just like John L. Sullivan on your side. The prize-fighter is employed in teaching the young Greek gods how to row. When they are not rowing in their boat, they all sit astride a bench and pretend to row, singing in chorus, while their leader takes the solo part. Then they all drink beer (don't tell William Platt this, or he will vote to repeal our Maine law) out of milk-cans. By and by the Oxford collegians, still in their blue vests and white pants, leave their tutor's manse and come to Formosa's villa at Fulham, where the Bishop of London lives. Formosa gives a most elegant party, but the Bishop is not invited, because Formosa—the program only gives her first name—is heterodox in her opinions. In fact, she is quite a vicious woman— a sort of Aspasia, I fancy, only not so literary. Though she never seems to go to Sabbath meeting, she has lots of young men waiting for her, as William Platt would call it; but I don't think they mean honourable. I don't quite understand this part of the piece; it is real difficult, dear mother, to get European culture all at once. Anyway, the leader of the Oxford collegians (called "stroke," but a stroke-leader is not the same as a strike-leader—I will explain this next mail) is a very unsteady young man. He drinks all day (I am right down glad William Platt can't do that in Maine) and plays euchre all night, and, I am sorry to say too, kisses Formosa in public. All this is what Oxford collegians, in their boating language, call "strict training." Fancy what a lot of trouble the author of the play, Mr. Dion Boucicault, must have taken to find out all these facts about the science of rowing. Towards the end of the play I began to fear that I should not see how the

Boat Race is rowed after all; for the stroke-leader loses all his dollars at euchre, and the sheriff (not Sheriff Augustus G. Harris, but another) comes to take him to the State Prison. But, luckily, his companions in the blue vests and white pants enter Formosa's parlor, where he is awaiting his trial, and rescue him from the police, so that the race takes place on time. Thanks to the strict training I have described, the stroke-leader wins, and the Oxford crew shake hands with the people in the crowd, hoodlums and all. Class distinctions are dying out in England, dear mother. But the reverence for authority is still as great as ever, for when the play was over the audience would not go away until Sheriff Augustus G. Harris had come forward to deliver an elegant oration.

I don't know much about the actors and actresses in the play, but they must all be real celebrated performers, because they have been promoted to the National Theater; and I suppose the only reason their names are not fixed up on the ceiling along with Garrick's and William C. Macready's is because they are not dead yet. The people in the pit and gallery treated what must be the flower of English acting very disrespectfully I thought— laughing at one of the players, a Mr. Harry Nicholls, before he opened his mouth, and even hissing two hardworking gentlemen who were the villains of the play. I do think it high-toned of the Sheriff not to have them at once expelled.

My money is lasting out very well, dearest mother. I don't need to go to Oxford now that I have seen what it is really like from Mr. Boucicault's play; and I guess I sha'n't pay for any more theater programs. Up to now they have cost me ten cents apiece, but I noticed that the young man in the next fauteuil to mine whispered "Press" to the attendant, and got his program for nothing. So I mean to whisper "Press," too, in future. Did I not contribute a column of "Yearnings for European Culture" to the *Bangor Independent* last fall? The Press in this country is allowed to do most anything. The young man next me slept through two acts of the play, and snored as loud as William Platt at Evening Meeting; and nobody dared to——

But here, as the young lady's remarks are getting personal, I break off. Somehow, her name sounds familiar to me. Can this be the same Miranda Hope, a selection from whose correspondence has already been published by Mr. Henry James? If so, I feel that she has degenerated under the influence of European culture; at any rate, I fear Mr. James may complain with justice that she has lost the purity of her American idiom.

THE NEW MELODRAMA.

"THE IDLER."

(St. James's Theatre, March, 1891.)

"ALL I want is four trestles, four boards, two actors, and one passion." So spake the elder Alexandre Dumas, contrasting the simplicity of his own dramatic method with Victor Hugo's weakness for mechanical "properties." Mr. Haddon Chambers, author of *The Idler*, is—in one respect at least—another Victor Hugo. He has a weakness for "properties." So important are they in his play that one suspects he bought them as a job-lot at an auction ("By Order of the Executors of the late M. Scribe"), and then wrote a drama for the purpose of utilizing them all. They would have served a Dutch painter for a good bit of still-life. On the floor is a bouquet. A fan lies on the table, and near it is a case of pistols, flanked by spirit-bottles, cut lemons, tumblers, cigars dry and green. The clock on the mantelpiece shows the hour of twelve, and at the back of the room are heavy curtains hiding a balcony. Let us take these "properties" and see if we cannot reconstruct Mr. Haddon Chambers's play out of them, for ourselves, by the method of Zadig.

You have not forgotten the episode of Zadig and the horse in Voltaire's story? "The finest steed in the royal stables had escaped from the hands of a groom into the plains of Babylon. The Master of the Horse asked Zadig whether he had seen the royal steed pass that way. 'You mean,' replied Zadig, 'a horse which gallops well; it has a small hoof; its tail is three feet and a half in length; the ends of its bit are of twenty-three-carat gold; its shoes are of fine silver.' 'Which way did it go?' asked the Master of the Horse. 'I have not seen it,' answered Zadig, 'and no one has described it to me.'" Then, you remember, the sage explained how he had reconstructed the horse from the various traces it had left in its passage.

Let us apply this ratiocinative process to Mr. Haddon Chambers's "properties." Our first guess is very easy. The pistols obviously mean a duel. But this is an English play, and ordinary Englishmen do not fight duels. The owner, then, of the pistolcase is either a foreigner (perhaps an American? Note the *green* cigars) or an Englishman who has sojourned in some country where pistolling is still practised. Our next guess is equally easy. The duel is about the lady of the bouquet and the fan. Is she virtuous? Clearly, because we are at the St. James's. But the juxtaposition of the fan and the whiskeybottles, lemons, cigars, etc., shows that the lady is in a bachelor's rooms, and the duel shows that somebody is entitled to be jealous of her presence there. We at once get our two combatants—the lady's husband and the bachelor (a would-be seducer, of course). A moment's thought, and we see that the fan is on the table to reveal the lady's presence to the husband. Where, then, is she hiding? Why, behind that heavy curtain at the back, necessarily.

But how to account for the presence of a virtuous wife in a bachelor's rooms? Remember, we have two *pièces justificatives* left, the clock and the bouquet. Obviously the clock won't help us much. Stage clocks always indicate the hour at which something catastrophic is going to happen. The fact that the hands of this clock are pointing to twelve shows that, like what the soldier said, it is not evidence; for twelve cannot be the hour of the lady's visit to the bachelor. A wife could not easily be absent from home at midnight, and the fan excludes the alternative hypothesis of twelve noon. The bouquet is more promising. It has been perfumed with a subtle poison by a jealous princess and sent to the lady—stay! that is *Adrienne Lecouvreur*. The bachelor has brought it in the absence of—no! that is *Divorçons*. Think again, and you notice the bouquet is on the floor. Then it must have been dropped, and dropped of course as a signal. Now bouquets on the stage are only carried at weddings, Drawing Rooms, and balls. This bouquet cannot have been dropped at a wedding, for the play is not *Le Chapeau de Paille d'Italie*. Nor at a Drawing Room, for it is not *The Cabinet Minister*. So the wife must have dropped the bouquet at a ball as a signal to some one —the bachelor, of course. Moreover, the signal obviously means that the lady consents to visit the bachelor's rooms. The husband must have been present at the ball, or signalling would not have been necessary. Hence we establish the fact that the husband and the bachelor are friends.

Let us now summarise the results which Zadig's method has yielded. A virtuous wife drops her bouquet at a ball to signify to a bachelor friend of her husband that she will pay a nocturnal visit to his chambers. There a fan betrays her presence to her husband, an Englishman who has acquired a knack of pistol-shooting in lawless countries (our first hypothesis, that he is a foreigner, is excluded by the consideration that English stage heroines never marry aliens), and who promptly proposes to exchange shots over the table with the would-be seducer. Up to this point, observe, Mr. Haddon Chambers's may be said to be an inevitable inference from the "properties" with which it starts. So far, it has invented itself. The first and only demand upon the playwright's own invention arises in that little matter of a motive for the wife's nocturnal visit to the bachelor. Even here Mr. Haddon Chambers prefers his inventions ready-made. Adapting the central situation of *Measure for Measure*, he sends the lady to the bachelor's rooms as the price for her husband's life, which the bachelor undertakes to save from a *dieu vengeur* whose brother the husband has been so unfortunate as to kill. By making the *dieu vengeur* an American, Mr. Chambers satisfactorily disposes of those green cigars. The only remaining "property" is the clock, indicating twelve, and that is utilized by appointing the duel for the stroke of noon.

The play is luxuriously mounted, and the players are faultlessly dressed at the St. James's, which is not conducted on the Dumasian principle of "four trestles and four boards." Indeed, so far as sumptuary details and Persic apparatus, generally, are concerned,

> They nothing common do nor mean,
> Upon that Alexandrine scene.

The acting, too, is excellent, as is only to be expected from a company which includes Mr. Alexander and Miss Marion Terry, Mr. Herbert Waring and

Lady Monckton, Miss Maud Millett and Mr. Nutcombe Gould. A real American has been imported to smoke the green cigars, a Mr. John Mason, who is astute enough to humour the Britishers by talking stage-American as though it were his native tongue.

"DIAMOND DEANE."

(Vaudeville Theatre, March, 1891.)

"OH, oui," says Mdme. Chaumont in *Divorçons*, "je suis une femme très respectée," adding something to the effect that the fate of being universally respected is not, for lively temperaments, all beer and skittles. Here, I suspect, Mr. Henry J. W. Dam, the author of *Diamond Deane*, may be of one mind with Mdme. Chaumont. His play has been too respectfully received. As a journalist, he was assured in advance of considerate treatment from fellow-journalists; and as an American who has elected to produce his first play in London, he might count on the indulgence of Londoners, flattered by his choice. But, being an intelligent man, he would probably have preferred to have his play taken on its intrinsic merits; which appear to me to be exactly those of a drawing-room melodrama of a conventional type. On the other hand, the play has appeared to Mr. Dam's friends as something much more ambitious than that—as a play with a scientific basis: a psychological (word more comforting, to a certain order of minds, than many Mesopotamias!) experiment, a "study in criminology." Where does the "criminology" come in? If anywhere, it must clearly be in the character of the eponymous heroine —a lady in league with a gang of thieves, who has earned her nickname by her skill in insinuating herself into the confidence of British matrons, in order that she may purloin their jewellery. Let us, then, examine the behaviour of this young person, with an eye to its "criminological" aspect.

There are two sides to the dramatic treatment of crime, as there are two sides to a tea-cup —the outside and the inside. If any one objects that this analysis is not sufficiently subtle for so scientific an affair as "criminology," I would point out to him that it has at least the merit of simplicity. And, perhaps, by the judicious use of index numbers, I may give it a properly scientific appearance. Thus:—

(1) The "outside" view of the criminal is that usually adopted in melodrama. You take your criminal ready-made, you provide him with plenty of cunning and resource, innumerable disguises, slow music in the orchestra, and you pit him against a detective, equally cunning and resourceful, own brother to M. Lecoq, warranted to say, "I think I have seen that face before," at any moment, and to identify all the personages in the play by reference to a note-book. In the contest of wits, the detective ultimately triumphs, and the play ends with handcuffs. That is the common "police drama." Needless to say, it has nothing to do with "criminology."

(2) The "inside" view of the criminal is, for obvious reasons, more common in novels than in plays. It admits us to the innermost recesses of the criminal's mind, shows us why he became a criminal, and, probably, why he is anxious to cease being one. Here we get more scientific, and may allow ourselves further subdivisions. Thus:—

(*a*) You may go in for paradox, and show that

crime is not always followed by either repentance or punishment. In short, you may controvert Mr. Gilbert's proposition that "The burglar's life is not a happy one," by picturing crime as leading to an easy conscience, wealth, longevity, troops of friends, and a Latin epitaph in Westminster Abbey. The best instance of this treatment which I can call to mind is M. Barbey d'Aurevilly's *Le Bonheur dans le Crime*, wherein a husband, after poisoning his wife with the assistance of his mistress, marries the mistress, and the pair live ever afterwards, in the author's words, "parfaitement heureux." But this method, not making for righteousness, is unsuited to a nothing-if-not-moral stage, which naturally prefers—

(β) The view that crime is its own worst chastisement. Adopting this view, the playwright, instead of showing his criminal as engaged in a game of hare-and-hounds with the police, has to present him as a *heautontimorumenos*, suffering agonies of remorse, and ultimately confessing his crime—not, of course, to the detective, but to some third person. This third person in Dostoievsky's *Crime and Punishment*—the archetype of this kind of story—is a young prostitute who quotes the Scriptures; in *Diamond Deane* it is an elderly parson, who quotes his own sermons. Mr. Thomas Thorne's parson is exceedingly tedious, and for my part I should have preferred the prostitute; but even Mr. Thorne's well-known readiness to undertake impersonations quite unsuited to his powers would probably have hesitated at that experiment. That, however, is a detail. The great aim of plays of this class is to inspire sympathy for the criminal, on the principle that "to understand is to forgive." We are to see how he could not help becoming a criminal, we are to be moved with pity as we watch his remorse gradually driving him to frenzy, and our nervous tension is to be relaxed along with his in the final scene of confession.

Something of this latter kind, no doubt, Mr. Dam

has aimed at in *Diamond Deane*. Miss Millward, as the ladylike thief, gives us the orthodox *apologia pro vitâ suâ;* she is a thief because her father was a thief, " and so," to quote Mr. Gilbert once more, " were her sisters and her cousins and her aunts." Miss Millward, too, duly wrings her (light-fingered) hands with remorse, and duly 'fesses, like Topsy, in the end. But the remorse is spasmodic, not cumulative; it does not gather momentum as the play proceeds; and the confession is not made, as it should have been made, to seem inevitable. It merely happens. There is a parson on hand, and the audience want to catch the last train to Brixton, so the confession is, if the colloquialism may be pardoned in connection with so high a matter as " criminology," " rushed " upon one. Moreover, Mr. Dam seems undecided whether his play is to be in class (1) or class (2) (β)—a mixing of categories which I, who have just invented them, cannot be expected to pardon. He introduces the Lecoq detective, notebook and all, and straightway we settle ourselves down for the dear old hare-and-hounds business of class (1). But, lo! the detective, instead of detecting, merely suggests to the parson that now is the time for a confession—and so we go off at a tangent into class (2) (β). Really, this is very confusing to a mind attuned, at the invitation of Mr. Dam's friends, to the pitch of the 'ologies.

The rest of the play is drawing-room melodrama —which, after all these years, is about as exciting a form of entertainment as parlour croquet. "Diamond Deane," in order to obtain possession of some valuable gifts intended for the mistress of the household which she has selected for the scene of her depredations, personates that lady by the simple device of borrowing her cloak and lace mantilla. This flimsy disguise—only to be permitted as a dramatic expedient in the romantic world of the Elizabethans—suffices to deceive the lady's husband, brother, and lover; and much domestic unhappiness results. Which of these three gentlemen was the most egregious idiot is a nice question that must be left—not, to be sure, for the experts in "criminology," but for the Commissioners in Lunacy to settle. Mr. Conway played the husband with an air of abject unbelief which seemed to show that he had already settled the nice question in favour of himself. In the character of the wife, Miss Dorothy Dorr, an American actress of handsome presence and of considerable histrionic endowment, made a first appearance on the London stage.

"FATE AND FORTUNE."

(Princess's Theatre, July, 1891.)

IT was a thought of Marcus Aurelius that "at first tragedies were brought on the stage as a means of reminding men of the things which happen to them, and that it is according to nature for things to happen so, and that, if you are delighted with what is shown on the stage, you should not be troubled with that which takes place on the larger stage." These words have often been meat and drink to me when bidden to sit out a melodrama. It is true that the Emperor spoke then of tragedy, but the greater includes the less. And it was his misfortune, not his fault, that melodrama had not yet been invented. If it had been, he would have found in it, no doubt, what I find—a useful exercise in Stoic philosophy. When I hear the cosmopolitan villain hissing his contempt for "you En-n-glish!" through his teeth, I recognize that he is only κατὰ φύσιν, according to nature, and, when he is ultimately killed in the tunnel by a canvas locomotive, my delight with what is snown on the stage teaches me not to be troubled with what takes place on the larger stage—*e.g.*, with my misfortune in just missing the last omnibus. "For you see," continues the Stoic philosopher, "that these things must be accomplished thus, and that even they bear them who cry out, 'O, Cithæron!'" On the melodramatic stage they do not cry out, "O, Cithæron" so much as "Oh, scissors!" or, "Oh, what a surprise!" but the moral is the same. In a good melodrama you see that these things must be accomplished thus.

And that is why Mr. James Blood's *Fate and Fortune* is not, to my mind, a good melodrama. His plot is not convincing. He does not make me feel that these things must be accomplished thus. I wish he, and, for that matter, all his fellows, could be persuaded to turn to and read up Aristotle's "Poetics." The original is rather tough, but cribs are cheap. It is a commonplace of the subject that Aristotle's treatise, though in form confined to Epic, Tragedy, and other high matters, is really a practical manual for the melodramatist. With a practical manual to hand, why don't our melodramatists use it? It is no use railing at melodrama. So long as there is a public to read about electrocutions, so long as there is a crowd to gloat over a street accident, so long will melodrama be with us—that is to say, for ever. There must always be an outlet for what M. Zola calls *la bonne grosse sottise publique*. But, if we can't end it, let us see that the melodramatists mend it. Let them study Aristotle, and thence learn the all-importance of plot.

Had Mr. Blood, for instance, been more of a clerk in Aristotle, I am sure he would never have been satisfied with the third act of his *Fate and Fortune*. He starts well enough. His cosmopolitan villain murders one gentleman by hurling him from the tower of a ruined abbey. Good. The villain then manages to get the good young man detected in what appears to be flat burglary. Good again. I feel, with the Stoic, that these things must be accomplished thus. But in the third act the villain suddenly flags in his villainy; he ceases, as the rowing men say, to put his back into it. We are told, to be sure, that he is laying a trap for the forlorn heroine. But the heroine is entrapped behind the scenes, where the villain remains during the whole of the act—a grave fault, for a villain who is not seen in melodrama practically does not exist. And Mr. Blood's plot sins not only in defect but in excess. It has loose ends, which the author forgets to pick up. For example, take that little matter of the good young man and the apparent burglary. The villain has been beforehand with the good young man in opening the iron safe. He has stained his fingers in red ink in opening it, has wiped them with blotting-paper, and thrown the crimson-stained fragments on the floor. "What is this?" says the detective, when his lynx-eye subsequently detects the blotting-paper. "Blood? No, red ink!" Of course you immediately fasten upon the red-ink stain as a clue; you feel sure that the detective is going to remember it till he finds more ink on the villain's hands, and then—in fact, you anticipate one of the most exciting chapters in the plot from that red ink. But the author disappoints you. He introduces the red ink business at one moment only to drop it the next. It is a false scent. Another fault in Mr. Blood's plot is its lavish employment of coincidence. I can believe, at a pinch, that the heavy father, the forlorn heroine, the cosmopolitan villain, the heroine's foster mother, the comic policeman, and a ticket-of-leave burglar might all happen to visit the same ruined abbey at the same moment. But that the ticket-of-leave burglar should be (Mr. W. S. Gilbert has made the word classical) burgling a house on the comic policeman's beat just as the heavy father is outside and the cosmopolitan villain, insulting the forlorn heroine, is inside, strikes me, in the vocabulary of our golden youth, as a little "too hot." I do not feel that these things must be accomplished thus.

Once more I would entreat Mr. Blood to study Aristotle's "Poetics." Not only will he there learn to better his plots, but to simplify his diction. It is time that villains ceased from asking heroines if they love "another," and good young men from soliloquising about the villain's "ulterior motives." Language of this kind is not κατὰ φύσιν, according to nature.

BURLESQUE.

(An Open Letter to an Irish M.P.)

MY DEAR SIR,—Talking on the first night of *Carmen up to Data* with a common friend about Gaiety burlesque, I learned that you had been to see the *Ruy Blas* of that joyous stage some fabulous number of times. Seventy times seven, I think it was; in fact, nearly every leisure moment you could snatch from your labours at Westminster you spent at the Gaiety. And the same evening I lighted on an entry in the diary of the MM. de Goncourt, which should interest you. " Le grand succès d'une pièce, à l'heure présente [*i.e.*, 1865], est de créer le *reveneur*; c'est-à-dire l'homme qui voit vingt fois 'Orphee aux Enfers.'" History repeats itself; and you are the *reveneur* of 1890. You have published an apology for your favourite amusement in the form of a letter addressed to our friend, which, being labelled "open," may, I take it, be discussed without breach of courtesy by a third person. I address you not without a sense of mortification, the natural mortification of a man blind to the fun which arrides his fellow-men. You enjoy, it seems, "a good laugh," at the Gaiety. I bethink me of that chapter in your favourite book (and mine), Florio's Montaigne, headed, "How we weepe and laugh at one selfe-same thing." And this good laugh of yours "makes," you think, "for edification." I would in all humility ask you: how? For I, too, would like to enjoy a good edifying laugh at the Gaiety. But, alas, I only laugh there on the wrong side of my mouth. How do you manage it?

You rejoice at the vogue of the Gaiety, because (and this, I suppose, is where the " edification " comes in) " where burlesque flourishes, there the drama flourishes as well." But our drama, as you know, does not flourish; and may I ask you where "burlesque" flourishes just now? You make, to be sure, the inevitable reference to Aristophanes. No discussion of burlesque would be complete without that. But I am sometimes inclined to suspect that those who make this reference have no more read Aristophanes than Mr. Dick had seen King Charles's head. Any such suspicion in the case of yourself, a scholar and a man of letters, would, of course, be an impertinence; I will only say that you and I have not read our Aristophanes in the same edition. As I read him, I hold the nearest modern equivalent to be Mr. Gilbert's topsy-turvydom *plus* the fantasy of a Shakespearean fairy play, *plus* the scenic, choral, and choregraphic background of a Drury Lane pantomime. You think him better represented by a Gaiety burlesque. Let us, for a moment, compare the two.

First and foremost, Aristophanes was a poet, and the Gaiety librettist is not. For instance, the address of King Hoopoe to the nightingale, in the *Birds*, is only comparable, for ravishing lute-strains of melody, for airy, delicate fancy, to the "Queen Mab" speech or the songs of Puck. The most rhythmic passage of Ruskin never portrayed the glories of *cirrus* and *cumulus* as they are portrayed in the *Clouds*. You have the candour to admit the absence of this "lyric strain" at the Gaiety. The poets laureate of that establishment are of the family of the poet Bunn. But let that pass.

Secondly, Aristophanes was a thinker, and the Gaiety librettist is not. He had clear and consistent views (high Tory views, as you are bound to regret) about the politics and society of his day; and to the logical, orderly development of each one of these views plays are in turn devoted. Four of them, as you will remember, were impassioned pleas for peace in an age of war. In two of them he "went for" the popular poet of his day, Euripides, and the popular philosopher of his day, Socrates. Two others discussed Women's Rights and the Socialist Millennium. What Gaiety burlesque ever ventures to approach the "height of this great argument?" And Astrophanes was a thinker not only in the motive but in the construction of his plays. The huge fantastic paradox with which each of these starts is developed with a meticulous, untiring ingenuity worthy of Sardou. Think of the story of the founding of the borough of Cuckooton-on-Cloud, and tell me in what Gaiety burlesque you find the coherence in incoherence, the unity of impression I find in that.

Again, Aristophanes was a literary parodist. I need not recall to you the parody of Pindar in the *Knights*, of an Æsopic fable in the *Birds*, of a Socratic dialogue in the *Clouds*, of the stock-situations of tragedy in the *Acharnians*. We have had excellent literary parody, too, in modern Parisian burlesque. You remember, for instance, how cleverly the Greek idea of ἀνάγκη, as shown in Homer's treatment of Helen's "fatal gift of beauty" is parodied by MM. Meilhac and Halévy in *La Belle Hélène*, with its burden of "C'est la faute à la fatalité." This, the quintessence of burlesque, the element which may make of it an effective weapon of dramatic criticism, is, to be sure, now and then discernible at the Gaiety by those who have the eyes to look for it. But how faint, how tentative, how poor a thing it is there! *Carmen up to Data* follows, pretty closely, I admit, the story of the opera, but (except in the mesmerising of Don José and in the tendency of the amorous, fickle heroine to salute every one with "Oh! what a nice young man!") never really caricatures it. I note an attempt, and only one, to parody the stock situations of drama—the assassination scene to wit. This you may compare, if you choose, with the parody of Euripidean tragedy in the *Mysteries*, where Mnesilochus finds that the baby he threatens to kill is only a dressed-up wine-skin. But that is all the parody you will find in *Carmen up to Data*. And if you could discern any parody of Victor Hugo in *Ruy Blas* your eyes were keener than mine. I think I know what you will say to this. You will tell me that the supreme function of Gaiety burlesque is not literary parody but criticism of life; that its aim is "actuality," adroit illusion to current events, and you will be able to find me this feature in Aristophanes. Even the *scie* or refrain of the Gaiety topical song you will show me anticipated in the Greek. There is, *e.g.*, a constantly recurring line in a dialogue of the *Women in Parliament*—"That's just what they will do"—which would make a capital ending for each of the topical verses sung by Mr. Lonnen and Mr. Arthur Williams. But this "topical" element in Aristophanes was a mere parergon, a side-wind, a back-hander; whereas it gives the whole momentum and impact of Gaiety burlesque.

And this brings me to my own theory of Gaiety

burlesque—for it seems that institution is now so important as to compel every self-respecting man to have some sort of theory about it. May I, in all diffidence, submit mine to your iudulgent consideration? From a passing allusion to the "Bouddha of Frankfort," I see that you have dipped into Schopenhauer. You will remember, then, that writer's examination of art, perhaps the most brilliant bit of analysis in the whole Schopenhauerian philosophy. You will remember that art is shown to be life *minus* the will-to-live. In art "the world as will has been eliminated, and the world as representation alone remains." Now, I venture to conceive a Gaiety burlesque as the ultimate triumph of the will-to-live over the art of drama. McDougallism, the Pelican Club, 6 oz. boxing-gloves, and all the other topical allusions which constitute the "common form" of a Gaiety burlesque, these are the "world as will," and they have ousted from the Gaiety stage the literary, the artistic element, "the world as representation." They have done this because we English are the great exponents of the will-to-live: we drive at practice, as Matthew Arnold used to say: we demand life (particularly that kind of life which is distinguished by inverted commas) before art. You will, I hope, admit that this little theory of mine is a handy, portable, waistcoat-pocket sort of article. When you have used it to explain Gaiety burlesque, it will still serve to account for the success of Mr. Frith's pictures and Adelphi melodrama. One serious defect it has. It will, obviously, not account for your own presence among the faithful of the Gaiety. As to that, I can only have recourse once more to old Florio (whom I have been lately re-reading in that dainty little edition of your editing): "a rhetorician of ancient times said that his trade was to make small things appeare and seeme great." Forgive me, my dear sir, if I suspect that, in your apology for Gaiety burlesque, you have, in merry jest, bound yourself 'prentice to that trade.

PIERROTICS.

"L'ENFANT PRODIGUE."

(Prince of Wales's Theatre, April, 1891.)

PIERROT, who has been luring all polite London to the Prince of Wales's, is every one's delight; and my despair. For he is too vast a subject for any man to adventure upon, single-handed. The moralist, the philosopher, the historian, the belle-lettrist might each contribute whole tomes about him, to form one monumental, encyclopædic work: *Pierroticon Biblion.* Every critic should aim at the Rabelaisian ideal, to be a Grand Abstractor of Quintessences; but how to abstract the quintessence of Pierrot, the elusive, the impalpable, the omnipresent? Shall I take him historically, and trace him from the impudent slaves of Terence, through the Scapins and Sganarelles of Molière, the Figaros of Beaumarchais, down to our own Fags, Trips, and Sam Wellers? Or shall I seek him in the print-shops, where he is to be found in every "state" of black-and-white since black-and-white was, from Callot to Gavarni, and from Gavarni to the ingenious M. Willette of the "Chat Noir"? Or shall I moralise over him as the Evangelist, the Carlyle with a difference, the Preacher of the Gospel of Silence, who practises what he preaches? Or shall I approach him through his famous incarnators, the two Debureaus, Hippolyte Petit, Paul Legrand? Or shall I try and disengage his significance as a complex type of humanity : at once greedy, selfish, a liar, a thief, a nympholept, good-humoured, sentimental, vicious, innocent ; an irresponsible little animal ; the eternal child in man?

No; I will simply conjugate him as a verb. *Pierro,* I am Pierrot. *Pierrabo,* I shall or will, &c. *Pierrem,* let me be Pierrot ; a Pierrot-critic. Ah ! if I could only be a Pierrot-critic, and *mime* this article for you, instead of writing it. How much shorter it would be, how much more lucid ! My face is daubed with flour, my eyebrows are corked, my lips rouged. I wear a black skull-cap, and a white doublet covered with big buttons. I stand rigid with my eyes fixed. By and by a smile steals over my face ; I clap my hands ; I pout my lips into a round O ; I cover them with my right hand ; I kiss it with a loud smack, and waft the kiss into the air. You at once understand that *L'Enfant Prodigue* of MM. Michael Carré *fils* and André Wormser gives me exquisite pleasure. Then I half-close my eyes and lean with my head on my hand, like the statue of Shakespeare in Leicester Square,— and you forthwith conclude that I am analysing my impressions, trying to account for the pleasure which *L'Enfant Prodigue* gives me. My face becomes more serious ; I frown ; I scratch my skull-cap ; I take my head between my hands and wag it,--whereupon you perceive that the innumerable philosophic and æsthetic problems suggested by *L'Enfant Prodigue* are becoming too much for me. But alas ! my powers as a pantomimist soon break down; I am no Debureau, or Courtès, or Jane May ; and I find myself compelled, after all, to explain in words (oh, cutting irony !) a drama which demonstrates the superfluity of all speech.

The entertainment at the Prince of Wales's has

come as a surprise to English play-goers, who have hitherto associated pantomime with rough-and-tumble Boxing Night fooling, the heartrending sight of Mr. Harry Payne squeezing a policeman into a wafer behind a door, and the smell of oranges in the pit of Drury Lane. *L'Enfant Prodigue* reveals it to us as one of the finest of the fine arts, delicate, meticulous, nicely adjusted to the most subtle gradations of emotion, polished *ad unguem*. One would have supposed, beforehand, that the gamut of dramatic gestures was severely limited. That Pierrot-prodigal has no appetite for his breakfast, that he is violently enamoured of Mdlle. Phrynette, the laundress, that his papa is angry and his mother grieved—one was prepared to find pantomimic expression compass effects so simple as these. What one really finds at the Prince of Wales's is, that pantomime, far from being the simple thing we had thought it, is extremely complex. Watch papa-Pierrot as he sits reading his *Temps*. A look of boredom culminating in a yawn shows you that he is at the political leader. Up and down go chin and eyebrow, and you see he is studying the rising and falling stocks in the money-article. Then a sly smile expanding into a broad grin, and ending in convulsions of laughter, tells you that he has lighted on a story with a double meaning. He passes the paper, with finger on the spicy paragraph, to Mdme. Pierrot, who at first reads with an air of vacuous innocence; then comes the conscious irrepressible smile, the blush, the turn of the head. In the end, you feel that you have read every line of that paper and know the exact point of the racy anecdote. *L'Enfant Prodigue* is all compact of such details as this, details so cunningly contrived as to flatter us with a pleasant sense of our own intelligence—when they do not terrify us (as in the scene of the father's impotent rage over his son's dishonour), or tug at our very heart-strings (as in the scene of the mother's hysterical joy over the prodigal's return). Of course, the music greatly extends the range of expression. Not a glance, not a twist of the finger, not a turn of the head, that has not its appropriate accompaniment, or rather its elucidation, in M. Wormser's score. Indeed, the music here and there bears the chief burden of the drama. I do not know, for instance, how Mdlle. Phrynette's refusal to listen to her elderly admirer, except on the condition of his offering her marriage, could have been briefly delineated in absolute dumb-show. But M. Wormser has only to introduce three bars of Mendelssohn's "Wedding March," and the trick is done! With a musical commentary of this adroitness, Mr. Sneer would have comprehended the full significance of Lord Burleigh's nod without the aid of Mr. Puff's exegesis.

Over and above the sheer delight of pantomime, over and above the pleasure one derives from the skill of Mdlle. Jane May and Mdlle. Zanfretta, Mdme. Schmidt and M. Courtès, there remains the amusement of finding even more in *L'Enfant Prodigue* than either its authors or its interpreters intend. There is a world of suggestion in the piece. Through M. and Mdme. Pierrot one sees the typical French *bourgeois* household, thrifty, orderly, fond of good cheer, not a little philistine. Through flour-bedaubed Pierrot one sees the old Biblical story, and the hero of many *Dames aux Camélias* and innumerable Adelphi melodramas. Through Phrynette one sees countless "free ladies" of the Second Empire spoken of in the Book of the Prophets Goncourt, and Homer's Circe, and (if you like) Mother Eve herself.

This recrudescence of pantomime is a sign of the times. The pessimists, especially the pessimists of tender years, who find that they have been born too late into a world over-weary, will see in it a proof of dramatic decadence. All old, or senescent, literatures, these will say, inevitably tend to one of two bad ends—the circus or pantomime. Do we not find, in decadent France, M. Edmond de Goncourt confessing in his diary that he cannot abide the playhouse, and finds his sole intellectual refreshment in the circus? And did we not, in our fourth-form days, read of Nero, in decadent Rome, causing the adventures of Europa, Leda, Pasiphae, and other ladies not to be mentioned within ear-shot of the Lord Chamberlain to be acted before him in pantomime? But we are none of us infallible—not even the youngest of us, as the Master of Trinity observed—and perhaps the youthful pessimists are wrong about pantomime. It may not be a symptom of decay, as they think, but, as the optimists contend, of rejuvenescence, of a healthy return to first principles in dramatic art. Diderot, an optimist of the optimists, was a firm believer in pantomime. He had a crafty way of making all actors pantomimists, in spite of themselves. Taking a seat as remote as possible from the stage, he would thrust his fingers into his ears, and then, to the astonishment of his neighbours, watch the performance with the keenest interest. "They could not refrain," he says in his "Letter on the Deaf and Dumb," "from hazarding questions, to which I answered coldly 'that everybody had his own way of listening, and that my way was to stop my ears, so as to understand better.'" Well, at the Prince of Wales's we may share Diderot's enjoyment without the necessity for stopping our ears, and rediscover for ourselves the truth which he enunciated (in a letter to Voltaire), "that silence and pantomime have sometimes a pathos that all the resources of speech can never approach." For, strange as it may seem when the grimacing, flour-besmeared, drolly attired Pierrot is in question, the dominant impression one gets from the Pierrot who is the eponymous hero of *L'Enfant Prodigue* is an impression of pathos, of the Virgilian "sense of tears in human things." A very human thing, indeed, is Pierrot, as played by Mdlle. Jane May. Pierrot is as human as Ally Sloper—and not so vulgar. He is as childlike and bland as the Heathen Chinee—and not so subtle. He is as weak as flesh, "if not weaker"—like the wooden leg of the gentleman in "Martin Chuzzlewit." He is—like Oswald Alving—an unscrupulous devotee of the *joie de vivre*. Though he breaks open Papa Pierrot's cash-box and wastes his substance in riotous living with the fascinating Phrynette, we bring him in innocent. A thing of ingenuous vices and involuntary virtues, we declare him irresponsible. Hate him we cannot. When he returns home (in the snow, of course), and Madame Pierrot takes him to her ample bosom, we drop a sympathetic tear; when Papa Pierrot is angry with him we are not surprised, but when Papa ceases to be angry we rejoice and are exceeding glad. In the end, we forgive him; for, "in forgiving him, we forgive ourselves." You see, he is so very human, and (this is a concession to the patriots) so very French. Who but a French prodigal would think of eloping with a *blanchisseuse?* Imagine Pierrot-Pendennis eloping with a Temple "laundress," if you can! And who but a French prodigal would think of retrieving his forfeited honour by enlisting in a passing regiment? *L'Enfant Prodigue*, in effect, is a debauch of French sentimentality; and the tears you shed will have to be recorded, like Miss Blanche Amory's, as "Mes Larmes."

But it is not all tears. There is humour in the piece—the broad humour of Papa Pierrot; the gentle humour of his spouse; the frolic humour of Phrynette; and the boulevard, or front page of the *Vie Parisienne*, humour of the amorous baron who supplants Pierrot in Phrynette's mercenary affections. All this humour finds its expression in dumb show—dumb show so delicate, so various, so persuasive, as to give a fresh significance to Hamlet's contempt for "words, words, words." The whole performance is a masterpiece of curious felicity.

THE ORPHEUS LEGEND.

IN OPERA.

*(Gluck's "*Orfeo,*' revived at Covent Garden, November,* 1890.)

IS criticism, as Jules Lemaître would have us think it, the art of enjoying masterpieces? Whether or no, I take a malicious delight in applying the method of that literary hedonist to the great masterpiece of Gluck—of Gluck called by the fatuous austere, and said by one more fatuous than the rest to have "preferred the Muses to the Sirens." What, then, is the peculiar charm of Gluck's *Orfeo* for the modern man? He shall find it, I promise him, as he shall find the charm of all fine art anterior to the birth of the historic sense, less in what the work presents (though that is much) than in what it suggests. It will not yield him the instant poignant sensations of a *Françillon* or a *Paris fin de siècle.* No. If he be wise, as well as modern, he will first envisage the beauty of its form, as Mr. Gilbert sings, "in a contemplative fashion and a tranquil frame of mind." He will next transpose the fable, modernizing it, habiting it in coat and waistcoat. Then, inversely, after bringing the fable to himself, he will go back to its distant origin, tracing in the work the deposit of each successive century. So shall the modern man soar through the ages like a god. There lies the profound interest of classics like the *Orfeo.* As their substance is much earlier than their form, they embrace immense intervals in the history of man, and picture, in layer upon layer, many civilizations. As an obvious sun-myth (Orpheus is the sun, Eurydice the dawn—the curious may pursue the inquiry for themselves) *Orfeo* is at least four thousand years old. Through Virgil it can count twenty centuries; through Gluck, something more than one. Jacques Offenbach brings it down to our own youth; and it dates from to-day by all that Virgil, Gluck, and Offenbach did not put into it, and that I detect in it all the same.

But your stage-manager cannot soar god-like through the ages. He must fix a date for *Orfeo*, and of course he has fixed a wrong one at Covent Garden. He should have carried his researches back to a certain August evening in 1774, when *le tout Paris* (except Marie Antoinette, kept at home by her mourning for her father-in-law) crowded the beautiful little Opera House of the younger Moreau in the Palais Royal to hear the Chevalier Gluck's *Orphée et Eurydice*, to wonder at the disappearance of the accompanist's harpsichord from the orchestra, and to note the introduction of the harp—played (for even then orchestras adopted the Thucydidean policy of φιλοκαλοῖμεν μετ' ἰυτελεῖας) not by a separate harpist, but by the first horn. Any adequate revival of Gluck's opera must include a revival of the associations of that night; for though the subject of the work is "older than any history that is written in any book," its form is the form of the late eighteenth-century Paris—the Paris of Marie Antoinette, Jean-Jacques, and Fragonard. What though the composer was a German and his librettist an Italian? Eurydice is an unmistakable *Madame la Princesse Eurydice*, who coquets modishly with the *Seigneur Orphée* on their way back from Hades. Love is a dapper little court-page. Is not the score studded with chaconnes, minuets, and gavottes? Wherefore a sensible stage-manager, taking his courage in both hands, should costume his shepherds and shepherdesses of the first act *à la Watteau;* and his *Eroi ed Eroine* of the Elysian Fields should wear over tunic and chiton the flowing perruque and balloon-panier of the other Champs-Elysées. This piquant incongruity is only faintly adumbrated at Covent Garden. Incongruity, to be sure, you find there. But it is the incongruity of short ballet-skirts in an opera written before Fanny Ellsler was born, and of "happy (male) shades" in the uniform of the Metropolitan Fire Brigade. Twice, however, the stage-manager has blundered into a truth—only to be reproved by still more blundering critics. The childlike and bland *Furie e Spettri*—true eighteenth-century Parisian demons—have only moved one gentleman to sigh for the mechanical terrors of the Lyceum Brocken, while another complains that Eurydice expires on a sofa. As if a Louis-Seize Eurydice would have consented to die on anything else!

Happily it takes more blundering than even modern stage-managers and their commentators can compass to spoil an *Orfeo*. It is a musical poem — not a poem set to music nor music fitted with a poem — of ravishing beauty. "I have endeavoured," Gluck wrote of his own principles, "to reduce music to its proper function: that of seconding poetry by enforcing the expression of the sentiment and the interest of the situations without interrupting the action or weakening it by superfluous ornament"; and of these principles *Orfeo*, from the noble dirge "Ah! Se intorno" of the opening to the glorious pæan "Trionfi Amore" of the close, is the perfect expression. I am not, therefore, going to ruffle our modern Piccinists by calling him the eighteenth-century Wagner, for I remember the fate of Jules Janin when he called the lobster the cardinal of the sea. Writing of the amateur performance of Gluck's work at Cambridge, a critic said that "only a woman of genius is wanted to make *Orfeo* a popular opera." He spake more truly than he knew. The woman of genius has come, and has popularized *Orfeo*. What Berlioz wrote of Madame Viardot-Garcia, the great Orpheus of thirty years ago, may be applied word for word to her successor of to-day, Giulia Ravogli: "She has all the special qualities that the part demands; thorough mastery of the music, a simple and severe style, an organ puissant and noble, profound sensibility, expressive features, natural beauty of gesture." Her pathetic pantomime in that delicious scene in the Elysian Fields wherein Orpheus, forbidden to use his eyes, seeks Eurydice by his sense of touch, is a thing no one who has seen it is likely soon to forget. Guadagni, the original Orpheus, was taught acting by Garrick. I like to fancy—and stranger things have happened—that something of Garrick's teaching has passed by continuous tradition into this piece of pantomime, and that Giulia Ravogli is thus unconsciously giving us back at Covent Garden what first emanated nearly a century and a half ago from Drury Lane. Tradition is certainly operative later on, for Giulia's manner of rendering the famous "Che farò," first *sotto voce*, kneeling by the dead Eurydice, then, after the second adagio, advancing to the footlights and letting the full torrent of despair burst out, is, on the evidence of Berlioz, a faithful replica of Madame Viardot's. No recent Italian opera season in England has given us anything half so fine as Giulia Ravogli in Gluck's *Orfeo*.

IN BALLET.

(Empire Theatre, June, 1891.)

I AM sometimes disposed to think that ballet is destined to be the great art of the future. Even our religious propagandists, as we have lately been told, have become corybantic. So it is in society. The passion for dancing is gradually passing from the amateur to the artist—from the drawing-room, whither "dancing men" more and more refuse to come when hostesses do call, to the stage, where the said "men," like the Oriental pashas that in spirit they are, get their dancing done vicariously at the hands (or rather, at the toes) of innumerable daughters of Herodias. The charm of these nineteenth-century Salomes at the Empire, the Alhambra, and elsewhere, is irresistible : were they to demand, for their dancing, the head of John the Baptist on a charger, I am sure there would be none among us so churlish as to refuse them. But at present, fortunately, they prefer to demand about 25s. per week from the management, and well, I think, they earn that modest guerdon. What augurs most favourably for the future of ballet is that it combines the intellectual with the sensual appeal—though by no means in equal proportions. So far as it consists of pantomime, of a story acted in dumb-show, the ballet is an intellectual art. So far, I say ; but, then, that is not very far. The real object of this sort of entertainment (however you may dissemble the fact) is the exhibition, under drapery discreetly indiscreet, of the female form divine. And that is why ballet will still survive triumphant when Homer, Shakespeare, Mr. Rudyard Kipling's Kiplingisms, and the Blondin Donkey are all forgotten. "Male and female created He them" is the key to many mysteries: among others to the art and mystery of the ballet.

And it gives us, also, I think, the clue to the superiority of our London ballets over most of those to be seen (*exceptis excipiendis* of course—*e.g.*, those at the classic home of ballet, La Scala) in the continental capitals. The plain truth is that our women—or at any rate (for one must beware, Mr. Herbert Spencer will say, of the bias of patriotism) our ballet-girls—are prettier and more shapely than theirs. This is not mere insular prejudice; for the foreigners themselves confess as much. At the Eden Theatre in Paris I have seen ladies in the front row of the ballet who might well have been grandmothers, such beldames were they, so deeply fallen into the sere and yellow leaf. I am still sometimes haunted by the recollection of a ballet I saw at Valencia, in Spain, in which the ladies concerned might have passed for the grisly furies of Æschylus without the trouble of "making-up" for the part. For a perfect ballet, then, you must have beautiful women; and they have got them for the ballet of *Orfeo* at the Empire. I know, of course, what discount must be allowed for the deception of the stage: the paint, the powder, the—spare my blushes!—the padding. And there is another kind of deception peculiar to the ballet stage; I mean that movement, that quasi-military manœuvring of women in serried ranks, which, by blending their forms and so confusing the eyes, gives a resultant impression of beauty which is probably not borne out in the case of any individual figurant. The effect is the same as that of one of Mr. Galton's "composite photographs": the whole is more beautiful than its parts. But when all is said, the fact remains that our English ballet girls are very fair specimens of English beauty—more suave and curvilinear than the little mouse-like "Grévin" type they have in Paris, yet as vivacious and agile; not so statuesque, perhaps, not so effective in repose, as the Italian *ballerina*, but much lighter of foot than she, and far more delectable in feature.

The ballet being so good as it is, one immediately begins to ask—out of a perverse desire, may be, for an unattainable perfection—why it cannot be made better. He who ventures upon the subject of *Orfeo* should cast the shoes from off his feet, for the place whereon he stands is holy ground. There is no more venerable legend than this in the whole of mythology. It began, no doubt, as I have said, as a sun-myth. Then it lost its cosmic significance, and became softened down into that pathetic love-tale which we find in Virgil. You remember how that runs? On her wedding morn Eurydice dies from the sting of a serpent. Her husband, with his all-compelling lyre, descends into Hades to beg her back from Pluto, who consents to restore her on condition that Orpheus does not turn to look at her before he has reached the upper air. Of course, the husband cannot help looking back at his bride, and so she dies once more— this time for good. Then Orpheus, in despair, spends his nights and days by the banks of a lonely river, crying on the name of "Eurydice!" till the jealous Mænads tear him to pieces, and throw his limbs into the stream. But the head floats, and as it is borne down the tide, the lips still murmur "Eurydice! Eurydice!" This beautiful legend has been sanctified for us moderns by its alliance in the last century with the noble music of Gluck, nor has it been dishonoured by its burlesque treatment in Offenbach's *Orphée aux Enfers*. Altogether, there is no theme more rich in associations, poetic, philosophic, scenic, and musical, than this one. Therefore, I say, it behoved the designers of the Empire *Orfeo* to go warily.

Well, I suppose they have so gone—according to their lights. I will not chide them for giving the legend a "happy ending," and restoring Eurydice a second time to the arms of Orpheus. The thing was inevitable, on the stage—as Gluck recognized before them. But my quarrel with them is that their ballet lacks unity of impression. There is one dominant note in the Orpheus story, the note of tender melancholy, the note which Gluck never fails to strike throughout his opera. At the Empire they begin on a scene of rejoicing, the elaborate nuptials of Orpheus and Eurydice. This is a false note; it spoils the unity of things. No doubt they will say, "Oh, we had to have the wedding, because of its spectacular advantages, procession, and so forth." But look at Gluck's opening scene! Eurydice is already dead, and Orpheus is standing, bent with grief, over her tomb, upon which groups of shepherds and shepherdesses come to lay garlands. Here is a spectacular effect, quite as good as any wedding processions, and with the additional advantage of striking the right note at the outset. Were the Empire people afraid of copying Gluck? Surely not; for in the next scene, that of the infernal regions, they have copied him very closely—and very wisely. For we have Signorina Malvina Cavallazzi slowly descending into Hades lyre in hand, just as Mdlle. Giulia Ravogli descends at Covent Garden in that wonderful duologue "Furie! spettri!" with its great plangent octaves on the word "No!" And Signorina Cavallazzi gives us the same pantomime, in the scene where Orpheus seeks to recognize his bride by touch, as does Mdlle. Ravogli; with the difference that she melodramatises what in Mdlle. Ravogli's hands is the perfection of delicacy and restraint. One or two other questions might be asked. As, why superfluous and very unclassical personages should be introduced into the classic legend—*e.g.*, the Spirit of Malignity, the Spirit of Fascination—for no other reason apparently than that occupation is wanted for Signor Cecchetti and Signorina Rossi? And why should so important a personage as Pluto be made to take a back seat? And why is Proserpine represented by a giantess? And why do the shepherdesses in scene i. wear comical little hats like button-mushrooms? But enough of carping at trifles. As ballet develops, we may perhaps hope to spiritualize its primary function as a beauty-show by adding to it a strain of poetry, the feeling for the ideal, the saving grace of the ethereal. But the time is not yet.

THE HISTRIONIC TEMPERAMENT.

PREJUDICE AGAINST STAGE-PLAYERS.

THE prejudice against players is a delicate subject, which the players themselves are, it may be discreetly hinted to them, somewhat too prone to discuss uncritically. At a recent dinner of the Actors' Benevolent Fund, the familiar grievance, it seems, was brought forward once more. Mr. Henry Irving declared the prejudice to be "ignorant," and passed some severe strictures on the so-called "theatrical missions" which trade upon it. Mr. John Hare added that it was "bitter and unreasoning," and was sarcastic at the expense of a certain popular preacher, " who, while he reviled the theatre, did not hesitate to transfer to the tabernacle the more rudimentary tricks and effects of the stage." Both gentlemen, doubtless, do well to be angry. They speak of what they know—of that particular form of the anti-histrionic prejudice which comes home to their business and bosoms. The active, outspoken opposition to the theatre is in the England of to-day mainly sectarian. But the prejudice exists, always has existed, in many other quarters than those in which it finds loudest expression; it is, indeed, common to all societies and to all times. Mr. Hare seems to have underrated its extent and its historic importance. He thinks it is confined to a particular sect, and does not "emanate from the churches where the traditions of culture and liberality have been embodied in a Liddon or a Newman." But what of the bishop, of Liddon's church, who confessed to Mr. Irving that he avoided the theatre because "he was afraid of the *Rock* and the *Record*"? What of the bishop, of Newman's church, greater even than Newman, who condemned acting as "the prostitution of a body purified by baptism"? The prejudice is not merely Christian. John Chinaman has no reverence for baptism, but he has decreed that the son of an actor (along with the son of the public executioner) shall be ineligible for the mandarinate. If only for its antiquity, the prejudice is venerable; it came in with Thespis his cart. I wish Mr. John Hare would take up his Plutarch, and read there how "Solon went to see Thespis himself, as the ancient custom was, act; and after the play was done, he addressed him, and asked him if he was not ashamed to tell so many lies before such a number of people." Mr. Hare might then turn to his Plato, and see, in the third book of the "Republic" how unworthy it is of a man to be always speaking in the person of others. After that, he would, I think, have a little more indulgence for the prejudice of Boanerges and his tribe, who after all are only expressing in a somewhat crude and violent form a feeling as old and as wide as the world itself. Actors are admired, applauded, highly rewarded, loved, envied, the objects of the most flattering (not to say the most impertinent) curiosity. Yet deep down in the hearts of most men there persists the feeling that to make a public show of yourself for money, to be always expressing ideas not your own, and emotions which you do not feel, to pretend in short to be what you are not—to clap a hump on your back and call yourself Richard the Third, as Johnson put it—is to violate the dignity of a citizen and a free man, to resign the "captaincy of your soul." You may consider this feeling Philistine, if you will; call it "ignorant" with Mr. Irving, "bitter and unreasoning" with Mr. Hare; but the point is that nearly all men, whether consciously or unconsciously, entertain it.

I am not defending the prejudice. I am merely trying to appreciate it. Why will not the actors do the same? Why will they not frankly accept the situation, and regard themselves—with a certain pride—as a class apart? They have no substantial grievance now, no inequality before the law. They are not *capitis diminuti* as the Roman players were. The only difference between them and other men is that they sacrifice their Ego, their features, complexions, their whole personality, in the cause of art, so that we may regard the marks their profession sets indelibly upon them as the *stigmata* of a sort of martyrdom. Yet instead of recognizing this difference, and glorying in it, they are perpetually trying to hide it, trying to make out that they are just as other men. So we hear them, as more speakers than one were heard at this charity dinner, congratulating themselves on their rise in "social position," and we have Mr. Hare complaining that any distinction should be made between them and men "who distinguish themselves in other branches of art." This means, I suppose, that they want to hide their motley under a court suit and the silly ribbon of some silly order; for of material rewards they reap nowadays far more than their brethren of the other arts. It means that they are becoming emburgessed, as the French say—desirous of merging themselves in the ruck of mere commonplace citizens, of being enrolled in the mandarinate.

So, in Paris their comrades have been clamouring for the Legion of Honour: Maubant and Febvre and others now sport the red ribbon, and Coquelin will not be happy till he gets it. Let them have these gewgaws, by all means. Let half a dozen of them be made K.C.B.'s, if they will. But let them not think that they can thus obliterate the fundamental distinction between actors and other men; a distinction of which the prejudice against them is a more or less unconscious—and, if they will only look at it philosophically, not unflattering—recognition.

One consolation, at any rate, they may enjoy. The prejudice against them ought logically to include, and as a matter of historical fact has until quite recently included, the practitioners of all the imitative arts. These are all "speaking in the person of others"— on paper, on canvas. It was not, of course, against the actor that the Platonic attack on Mimesis (here Mr. Hare must again refer to his "Republic," Book III.) was primarily directed—though it touches him most nearly—but against the poet, or, as we should now say, against all fiction. So that the dramatist, the novelist, the painter, are all tarred with the same brush as the player. Yet here again it is well to distinguish. Among artists the obvious *differentia* of the player is that he is his own materials, his own paint and canvas, his own ink and paper. One wonders whether the constant simulation of emotion may not— looking at the results in the somewhat analogous case of fictitious feeling under hypnotic influence—occasionally impair the faculty for genuine feeling. The character of hypnotic patients who exhibit emotions under external suggestions, is in the end, it is said, sensibly deteriorated. Does not the actor incur some small part at least of this danger? Do we not

238 THE HISTRIONIC TEMPERAMENT.

find a true and uncomfortably suggestive type of histrion in Daudet's Delobelle, who, even when following his daughter's body to the grave, could not forget the gallery, and posed with his pocket-handkerchief, though the tears he shed in it were sincere enough? Dangers there are, then. But the true histrion can afford to face them, and the best of actors—one honours them for it—make their pride in their profession a family affair. Coquelin *aîné*, for instance, is now the firm of Coquelin *père et fils*. It is pleasant to find that Jean Coquelin can imitate his father to perfection in some of his father's very finest impersonations. The great Molière tradition at the Français, it is clear, is still safe—

Uno Coquelino avulso non deficit alter

—though, happily, no member of this family of brilliant comedians is as yet snatched away. One is glad to find good actors stoically abiding by their calling, in despite of their groans over the prejudice against it. Already we have a second generation of Coquelins, Terrys, Hares, Irvings, upon the stage. After all, this is the best practical refutation of old Plato and his "Republic," Book III.

SARAH BERNHARDT.

(*July*, 1889.)

MDME. SARAH BERNHARDT is off once more to the two Americas, and there is a sentence of Carlyle's (is it in " Sartor Resartus "?) that is ringing in my ears : "Your America is here, and now!" I cannot help wishing that some modern Frenchman with the authority and prestige of Carlyle (why not M. Renan? He is the pink of gallantry to actresses, and once had a legendary interview with a *café-chantant* songstress) would say to Mdme. Bernhardt : "Your America is here, in the Rue Richelieu !" In other words, one cherishes the hope that Mdme. Bernhardt may be persuaded to return to the Comédie Française. I know it will be said, "What business is that of yours? What have you, a Londoner, to do with the future movements of this French actress?" Well, in the first place, it is always agreeable to offer disinterested (and unsolicited) opinions about matters that are not one's own business. But I have a better answer than that : we Londoners happen to have a special interest in the vexed question of Mdme. Bernhardt's return to the Comédie. For it was we Londoners who were the primary cause of her leaving it. To speak strictly by the almanac, Mdme. Bernhardt's open rupture with the Comédie Française dates from 1880. But it was the extraordinary, the exaggerated, the unreasoning fuss that was made over her in London in the previous year that suggested to her soul to become like a star und dwell apart. It was the Gaiety French Play season of 1879 that turned Sarah Bernhardt into Sarah Barnum.

What has happened to Mdme. Bernhardt and her talent in the ensuing decade has shown Londoners how much they have to answer for. I am not thinking of the personal aspect of the matter: of the lady's strange adventures by land and sea, her pyrotechnic displays, her quarrels, her freaks, her advertisements. All these things she might have perpetrated, and welcome, for they need not have hurt her talent—are, indeed, only the defects (if defects they must be called) of her qualities. It is a commonplace of the subject that the ordinary rules about the conduct of life do not apply to players of genius: the moral writ of Islington or Peckham Rye does not run in Bohemia. It is not the lady's escapades that are here in question, but the strain upon the actress's talent, the wear and tear of her artistic personality; and, what is more, the evil effect her flight from the Comédie Française has had upon the stage at large. Let me take the last point first. If Madame Bernhardt's ten years of independence had left her talent absolutely intact, it would still be chargeable with having caused the production of many bad plays. Is it necessary at this time of day to point out that *Fédora*, *Théodora*, and *La Tosca* (leaving rubbish like *Léna* entirely out of the account) are not works of art, but pieces of mechanism? Who says art says organic growth: these things were constructed to pattern. They are vehicles for one and the same personality, mere strings of situations conditioned by that personality: not real plays—which show character and circumstance, passion and duty, will and destiny, brought to the grapple. There is no need to labour the point. It is sufficient to note that Mdme. Bernhardt's flight from the Comédie has spoiled Sardou. It has degraded the author of *Patrie* and *La Haine* into the contriver of *La Tosca*.

To pass on to the actress. The obvious disadvantage to her of her career of independence is that it has led her "to abound," as her countrymen would say, "in her own sense," to indurate her manner into mannerism, to burlesque herself. Heaven forbid that she should not be herself! In fact, Heaven has forbidden it, in her case as in the case of each one of us. The Sybil and the prophets, as Goethe says, have declared that mortal never shall escape himself.

> So musst du sein, dir kannst du nicht entfliehen
> So sagten schon Sybillen und Propheten.

And in following out the line of her destiny she has certainly given us a new type (new, that is to the stage) which one would not willingly have missed. I mean her embodiment of Oriental exotism: the strange, chimæric, idol-woman: a compound of Baudelaire's Vierge du Mal, Swinburne's Our Lady of Pain, Gustave Moreau's Salome, Leonardo's enigmatic Mona Lisa. Had she stayed at the Comédie, we should probably never have had this: it is the one distinct gain that has accrued to art from her "abounding in her own sense." But at what cost has she given us this! The essence of the type is a sort of nightmarish exaggeration, something not in nature, the supreme of artifice. To "create" a stage-type that is nothing if not exaggerated, unnatural, artificial, what a danger for the artist! What a risk of falling into mere trickiness! And it is but too certain that Mdme. Bernhardt has now developed tricks. For example, take her three favourite styles of delivery:

1. The rhythmical chant, or intoning; the sigh of linked sweetness long drawn out. This used to be admirable in *Phèdre*, and the cloying verse of Racine generally; admirable, too, when she played Marie de Neubourg in *Ruy Blas*. In *Théodora* it becomes burlesque.

2. The hammering out of her words, like pieces of metal; as the Lord High Executioner of Titipu would say, "with a short, sharp stroke." (For analogous musical effects compare "The Anvil Chorus," or "The Harmonious Blacksmith.") Of this the great instance used to be the passage in Act iii. of *La Dame aux Camélias*, in which Marguerite describes to Armand the seamy side of her life: the passage ending in the words "ruine, honte, mensonge." What a trick this has now become we have all heard in *Jeanne d'Arc* at the line "La France renaîtra."

3. The rapid patter. The words tumbled out, one over the other, at such a helter-skelter pace that one is simply left to gather their sense from the context, or the accompanying gesture. This went very well in the earlier acts of *Frou-Frou*, say, where, moreover, it was artistically right because it illustrated the character. But when I heard the same trick in the first act of *La Tosca*, it seemed to me mere incomprehensible gabble. An attempt to "break the record," only fit to be timed by a stop-watch, and accompanied by official starters, a referee, and a posse of sporting reporters.

As with her diction, so with her gesture and "business." One is conscious of general coarsening; a blurring of the outline ; an absence, every year more conspicuous, of what the three Miss Poles were fond of calling the Fine Shades. To be sure, her gesture is still, as it always has been, a thing of perfect suavity ; her postures are grace itself. Here at any rate is a little matter in which Mdme. Bernhardt might profitably instruct Miss Ellen Terry, with her favourite auctioneer arm and didactic forefinger, or Miss Ada Rehan, with her trick of shuffling off the stage with her toes turned in. But even here one cannot be blind to certain exaggerations. Her sinuous, serpentine way, for instance, of coiling round Maurice de Saxe or Cavaradossi, in the love scenes : is not that well-known Bernhardtian effect now somewhat over-done? No wonder the closely-hugged *jeune premier* sometimes looks a little embarrassed ! I suspect he goes off to the wings to comb his hair and smooth out his collar with a feeling of relief. And then the tricks of "business," and the game of hide-and-seek behind the colossal fan in *Fédora* and *La Dame*, the—but here let me cease the ungracious task of enumerating the spots on the sun. I only began it out of sheer weariness of hearing Aristides always called the Just. The perpetual pæans in praise of Mdme. Bernhardt would be much more effective for a discord or two.

To conclude, I suspect she herself understands the risks of "abounding in her own sense" quite as well as any of us could tell her. She knows her talent needs refreshing, revitalising, rejuvenating : witness her recent efforts to abandon the Vierge du Mal type in favour of a more orthodox kind of virgin—Ophelia, Joan of Arc, nay, even *the* Virgin. The flippant declare that she has only tried these parts just as M. Zola wrote *Le Rêve:* out of a mere casual desire to show that, like Todgers's, she can do it when she chooses. For my part I prefer to ascribe this new departure of hers to method rather than to whim: to her consciousness of a need for a larger, saner, more varied repertory. But she will never get that repertory so long as she goes wandering from pole to pole, with a new piece, specially constructed for her by M. Sardou, in her pocket. Only at the Comédie Française, with its tremendous range of plays, old and new, its discipline, its equality, its subordination of player to play, will she find the tonic refreshment her talent needs. Let her adopt the motto of another (but immeasurably inferior) comedian: poor Boulanger's "Je reviendrai."

CÉLINE CHAUMONT.

A MAN need not be the dupe of his impressions. Neither can he always master them. Why, as I sate the other night listening to Madame Chaumont singing "La Première Feuille," my thoughts should have wandered to one of Alphonse Daudet's minor sketches I cannot tell. Nor do I know where, or how, I had come across that little sketch. All I remember is that it was an "impression" of Déjazet, not the Déjazet that our grandfathers and great-grandfathers knew, but Déjazet in her extreme old age, the ghost of her former self. It was a hot August evening at Trouville. Daudet and his friends were discussing the Gallic equivalent for Shakespeare and the musical glasses, while a luckless pianist was trying to make himself heard above the din of conversation by playing "O Richard! O mon roi!" in *fff* octaves. Then a still small voice was heard at the window asking "May I come in?" and a faded little figure in a faded little gown marched into the bright circle of the lamp-light. It was Déjazet. They brought her to the piano, and there in a faded little voice she sang them a faded little ballad of Béranger, then a curtsy, and she vanished again into the blackness of the night. A few months later she was dead. A wonderful woman in her time —her time was from 1797 to 1875, from the Directoire to the Third Republic—but untoward fate compelled her to lag superfluous on the stage, when she should have been at home in her arm-chair, tended by her great grandchildren. She was playing at the Vaudeville in the spring of the very year of her death.

Why did I think of all this as I sate listening to Madame Chaumont? She is not old (heavens! do not suspect me of any innuendo so ungallant as that) nor does she lag superfluous. Was it because Madame Chaumont has been called a second Déjazet? Was it because Madame Chaumont's voice (for reasons, however, that have nothing on earth to do with the lapse of time) has become almost as faded as Déjazet's? Or was it because the half-curious, half-reverent mood of the audience listening to the faded " Première Feuille," seemed to me like that of the little circle at M. Daudet's listening to the old-world " Lisette " of Béranger? Madame Chaumont still sings her famous song with exquisite finish and delicacy, still sings it with that true intonation which is the surest evidence of a fine ear; but where is the voice? *Où sont les neiges*—no! that quotation, I fear, is a little faded too. Musically considered, this famous song, I fear, is trash. Here are a few bars:—

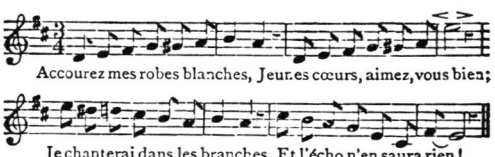

Accourez mes robes blanches, Jeunes cœurs, aimez, vous bien;
Je chanterai dans les branches, Et l'écho n'en saura rien!

with simple tonic-and-dominant harmony, *tum-ti-ti, tum-ti-ti*, as you perceive. But my dear Brixton Angelina, when you try this over at your piano, as I know you will, don't turn up your nose at it until you have been to hear it sung by Madame Chaumont. (By the way, don't tell mamma when you get home. Say you have been with Edwin to Exeter Hall.) Observe the songstress's facial play throughout these eight bars: the little encouraging smile at the

"Accourez mes robes blanches"

(you, of course, are the "robe blanche"), broadening into a sort of maternal expansiveness at the

"Jeunes cœurs aimez-vous bien"

(the "jeunes cœurs" are yours and Edwin's, you know), then the change to a face of cheerful—what shall I say?—detachment, know-nothingness, at the

"Je chanterai dans les branches"

(as much as to say, "Don't mind me, young people. I shall be singing in the branches, but I shan't look"), followed by a discreet, demure drop of the eyelids at

"Et l'Echo n'en saura rien,"

—and I hope mamma won't, either, when you get back to Brixton.

What there is left of Madame Chaumont's singing-voice is pleasant enough, but of her speaking-voice what can one say? Frankly, that seems to me, perhaps, the most disagreeable voice now to be heard on any stage. Yet the actress triumphs over it—nay, even triumphs by it. You know, of course, the immense importance of the voice to the player. Think how much of the charm of the Terry family depends on the Terry voice; how much of the charm of Sarah Bernhardt's on hers. Some critics have held voice to be more necessary to an actor than histrionic power. The Greeks held this view to a man. Demosthenes said that "actors should be judged by their voices." And Plato would expel " the actors with their beautiful voices " from his ideal state. Madame Chaumont would be safe from expulsion on that score, at any rate. Her normal tone is a sing-song, of the sort adopted by children when they are asked to recite " The boy stood on the burning deck" before visitors. This is varied by curious nasalities (the *voix canaille* of the Parisian street arab), by sudden little squeaks, and by frequent descents into the raucous bass of the cabman whose vehicle has been standing too long outside the public-house. Yet this strange, repellent voice is a good half of Madame Chaumont's success. Why, I cannot guess, unless it be owing to the piquant contrast between the vulgar tones and the sumptuous, yet elegant, costumes of the little lady who utters them.

But we have not yet pierced to the true inwardness of Madame Chaumont's talent. She is immensely, amazingly, diabolically intelligent. You feel that she understands everything; that, like the Master of Balliol in the undergraduate's rhyme, she may boast " What I don't know isn't knowledge." This, no doubt, comes partly from a long and varied experience (she first came out in 1863 as the *rosière* in Feuillet's *Montjoye*, and since then " has seen many men and cities, and known their minds "), but it must come, too, from great natural brain-power. And this intelligence manifests itself, as intelligence on the stage always will, in minute, elaborate, continuous pantomime. She acts with the palms of her hands, the tips of her fingers, her toes, the nape of her neck, the small of her back. Her silence is more expressive than most people's speech, her face going through as many queer contortions in five minutes as the features of a convict who objects to having his photograph taken. Then she has tricks of gesture which are all her own : a rapid series of taps with one foot (imitated by the divine Sarah, and clumsily imitated, in the first act of *Frou-Frou*), a way of crossing the stage with a glide and a duck, her own peculiar wink, her own peculiar shrug. Unfortunately —it is the old story—she now exaggerates her pantomime. Vivacity has at last become a something dangerously like St. Vitus's dance. And she underlines every point, forces the meaning down your throat, irritates you as a page all italics irritates. This excessive emphasis is all very well when the actress is dealing (as her authors take good care that she generally shall be dealing) with double meanings. But a play (not even a Palais Royal or Variétés play, whatever some English prudes may think) cannot be all double meanings. There must be intervals of single meaning, and even of no meaning, and these intervals are Madame Chaumont's *mauvais quarts d'heure*—and her audiences'.

In this matter of delivering double meanings, it is the fashion to compare Madame Chaumont with Madame Judic. But the methods of the two are essentially different. The one underlines with a glance fraught with mischief what the other, all innocence and unconsciousness, lets drop with wide-open surprised eyes. It was Paul de St. Victor who said that Judic used a fig-leaf as a fan. Chaumont takes it up, dissects it, crumples it, destroys it. The result, the cynic may be disposed to observe, is much the same.

In neither case is that useful piece of foliage allowed to serve its proper purpose of a screen. But the philosophy of fig-leaves is too great a subject to be lightly broached here,

" Et l'Echo n'en saura rien "

from my lips.

COQUELIN *AÎNÉ*.

M. GOT once told a Curious Impertinent that in the long-run brains were of more harm than good to an actor. This deliverance may have been intended by M. Got to encourage this common (or Conservatoire) histrionic aspirant. Or it may have been, like Coleridge's metaphysics in the opinion of Lamb, only his fun. Or, again, it may have been a covert gibe at Coquelin *aîné*. For behind that comic mask of his—restless, twinkling eyes peeping from under fleshy lids, flexible gash of a mouth, "trumpet" nose, heavy muzzle: the traditional comic mask, the mask of David Garrick and John Liston, of Frances Abington and Marie Bancroft—Coquelin *aîné* has brains. And the brains have sometimes stuck the mask on the wrong dummies. For brains beget theory, and theory begets malpractice. One of Coquelin's theories is that there is no such thing as a stage *emploi*: that an actor, if only he have the mind (doubtless in the double-edged sense of the familiar story about Wordsworth), can play any part. And, accordingly, one of his malpractices has been to play heavy fathers like the elder Duval in *la Dame aux Camélias*, sentimental young fiddle-makers like *Le Luthier de Crémone*, elegant men-about-town like Gondinet's Brichanteau. Now, the injunction against poking your nose into other people's business has peculiar force when the business is stage-" business" and the nose is Coquelin's nose; and he of all men should never have neglected the homely advice to follow that organ if you want to go straight.

Yet his first attempts to follow it would appear, from some scraps of anecdotage collected by M. Francisque Sarcey, to have been only half-successful. "Oh, no; the boy is too ugly!" said Augustine Brohan when Coquelin was a candidate for admission to the Conservatoire: "look at his trumpet nose!" "And he uses it like a trumpet," added Auber unkindly. The truth is that at that time he spoke through it. So the jury were for rejecting him. But Régnier, with an eye for that nose and for the mask in its background, took its owner into his own class. Régnier was a great actor, but he was a still greater professor. He found young Coquelin mistaking, as beginners will mistake, exuberance in gesture for significance and turbulence for gaiety, and equipped with a voice too often betrayed by those inopportune squeaks which English clarinet players call "goose." Discerning here a Scapin in the rough, the teacher set his pupil to practising not the Scapins but the Gérontes. Three months' penitential incarceration in the comic elder's sack qualified the youngster for administering Scapin's *coups de bâton* himself. He had learned to moderate his transports. He was already in a fair way of becoming the Coquelin that we know: the finest exponent this century has seen of the Mascarilles, the Scapins, and the rest of the brilliant and irresistible *valetaille* of Molière.

But it was as a valet of Beaumarchais that he first took the town by storm: as Figaro—not the Figaro of *Le Barbier* but the Figaro of *Le Mariage*, the Figaro of the monologue; Alexander the Great, not Alexander the Coppersmith. It seems to have been a fashion just then at the Français to give a tragic twist to the comic characters of the classic repertory. Old Provost had begun the game by making Arnolphe a serious and "sympathetic" personage. Coquelin tried this process on Figaro by acidulating the soliloquy, giving it something of the fuliginous hues and, if you like, a note or two of the first rumblings of the proletarian volcano. It was Figaro-Danton and even Figaro-Schopenhauer—a trick, of course, but a trick that fairly caught all Paris. And now Coquelin was allowed to follow his nose to its proper destination, the world of Molière and Régnard, where the valets never cease from troubling and their masters are not at rest. He took all the joyous, intrepid, flamboyant, splendidly mendacious figures of classic buffoonery in turn—Mascarille of *Les Précieuses* and *l'Etourdi*, Scapin of *Les Fourberies*, Crispin of *Le Légataire*, and the rest of their rascally tribe—and made them his own. His comic valet is not, as Régnier's was, a piece of subtle, delicate, filigree work, but a creation large, solid, robust. His Scapin is massive and concrete, like Mr. Wopsle's Hamlet, and with better excuse. His Mascarille is a monument *ære perennius*—in this connection to be construed more lasting than Mascarille's own brass. These twain present you the epic of fantasy, the ridiculous raised to the sublime. He plays them, Mr. Henry James has said, as though Molière were prompting him from the wing. His method here is the wholesale method, the method of laying it on with a trowel, the method of "large maps." He delivers his long speeches all in one breath, straight out from the chest, caring little for the fine shades but very much for the general impression, for the momentum and impact of the thing as a whole. There is, for instance, the long speech in *l'Etourdi*, a speech of over two hundred lines, a good half of which is next to unintelligible. It used to be a tradition at the Comédie to deliver the thing in *tempo rubato*, dwelling with emphasis on one or two of the more animated passages and slurring over the rest. Coquelin takes the whole in one big rush, *prestissimo*, and, as one of his critics has put it, overwhelms his audience with an avalanche of Alexandrines. And while Coquelin has repeopled for us one "hemisphere of the great globe of Molière," there are tracks in it which he may be said almost to have been the first to explore. Before his advent, who suspected that Monsieur Loyal, the catchpoll in *Tartuffe*, was anything more than a mere super? M. Sarcey recollects—for the actor no longer condescends to characters of that rank—that it became in Coquelin's hand a distinct and original "creation." Londoners have often had the opportunity of seeing for themselves what he makes of the single hint "etc." at the close of the impromptu in *Les Précieuses*.

In the modern repertory there are two Coquelins, the old and the new; and there are (the actor himself is not one of them) who say that the old is the better. The old is the successor of Régnier, whose parts the pupil has appropriated by right of inheritance. Coquelin's Destournelles, his Oscar, his Colombet, his Julien, have all been gratefully received by the young generation; but the old fogeys have found the pupil lacking in the variety and delicacy of the master. Elisha must expect to have Elijah thrown at his head. In the new Coquelin you have the outcome of a revolt of the brain against the nose, of the mind against the mask. It is the old story. Liston pined to play Hamlet; and the man whom Nature specially created to play comic valets burns to figure as lovelorn musicians or as the personified sentimentalities of Octave Feuillet. He longs to conquer the heart of the Lowther Arcadian *ingénue* and to compel other tears than tears of laughter. True, he has proved himself able to do these things; but others can do them as well or better. Worms is held to surpass him in his pet Chamillac. A second-rate actor followed him in the part of Brichanteau, and was not, we are told, inferior. Caprices like these serve to justify Got's sarcasm about the danger of brains in an actor. The danger, it seems, is not yet passed. Scapin has lately been casting a too roving eye on "heavy leads." He essays to show us a new Tartufe, a new Alceste. Again there are who say the old is the better.

The theatre has not sufficed him. Coquelin the comedian of the Rue Richelieu has another self in Coquelin the reciter of the Faubourg, where he gives up to five o'clock party what was meant for mankind. In this way he has introduced a few poets, and poetasters not a few, to the notice of the great— Banville, Alphonse Daudet, Bouchor, Paul Delair, Lenormand, and many *quos numerare non oportet.* There yet remains another Coquelin—Coquelin the critic, the literary polemist, the apostle of the Diderotian paradox, the essayist who discusses histrionic theory with a pretty little style of his own. His enemies have hinted that it is not his own, but a "ghost's." But call on Coquelin at any time before rehearsal hour in the morning, and you shall find his desk littered with "copy" in his own microscopic handwriting. And take care—or he will read it to you.

HENRY IRVING.

IT is no longer modish to deal in universal categories. Time was when you commenced aphorist by compelling the whole human race to choose alternatives of your invention. " All men are either—," you began brazenly, and tossed up a coin to determine the predicate. Born Aristotelians or Platonists, said one; borrowers or lenders, said another. Fools or d——d fools, suggested the undergraduate. Of such dead-and-gone dichotomies there is one, a favourite with the French Romanticists of the Thirties, which might well be revived. Théophile Gautier and his generation divided mankind into the two great classes of *flamboyant* and *dreb*. Don Quixote, Diderot, Shelley, the Devil (Milton's, of course), and Mr. Henry Irving, are all flamboyant. Sancho Panza, Voltaire, Wordsworth, the "magnified Lord Shaftesbury" of Matthew Arnold, the British Public, are all drab. It is the glory of Mr. Irving that he gives the world the spectacle, all too rare, of the two classes in their proper relationship; that is, the second subservient to the first. A flamboyant of the flamboyants, he has conquered the drab public. Don Quixote has brought Sancho to heel.

In the great Reckoning Day of the arts, this shall be counted unto him for righteousness. He has vindicated the supremacy of Romance in the face of all Philistia. The assertion is not to be carped at as

only a roundabout way of saying that he is a romantic
actor who has won the favour of the pit. Merely to
call him a romantic actor might mean little enough;
the phrase has been too often used on the stage—
where even the great name of romance has not escaped
degradation—for some little extra smirching of red
ochre and burnt cork; a mere difference between
"twopence coloured" and "penny plain." The
point is that he is a flamboyant, a romantic in the
grand style, drums beating and colours flying. He is
a dreamer of dreams, the Alnaschar of the stage—
yet happier than Alnaschar in that his most splendid
visions, "the cloud cap't towers, the gorgeous palaces,"
become for us all, in due time, waking realities on the
Lyceum stage. Like his own Charles, in Marvel's
verse, he nothing common does nor mean upon that
memorable scene. At his worst, as at his best, he
ever touches the imagination. Now, to touch the
imagination in the playhouse world of Romance and,
withal, to bring the great outer Philistine world to its
knees—to set our ears ringing with the "chink-chink"
of the Polish Jew's sleigh-bells, and to get elected to
the Athenæum Club *honoris causâ*—is an achievement
verging on the paradoxical; it is running with the
hare and hunting with the hounds. Alone among
actors, Mr. Irving has taken this double-first: a
success on the stage and off it—*in republicâ tanquam
in scenâ*, as Lord Coleridge once said of him in the
words of the great Roman orator. Of his pre-
decessors, Macready came near doing it, but failed.
For Macready was a bit of a Philistine—was, in fact,
among the drabs. He was ashamed of his profession.
Mr. Irving is proud of it, feeling a stain on its honour
"like a wound." Burke's phrase comes naturally to
the mind, for there is something chivalric in the man

as in the player—a dignity, a gust, a touch of the hidalgo.

When a quarter of a century ago Henry Irving, after ten year's rustication, was permanently enrolled in a London company, the prospects of the English stage were, as Mr. Stevenson would say, aleatory. The die might have come down drab; our next great actor might have been a John Kemble or an elder Farren, a classic, a depositary of "correctness" and the traditions. Like every other young actor, Irving began by doing what Théodora, in Sardou's play, says her imperial husband does—*un peu de tout*. Of these miscellaneous experiments, our elders still profess to remember with gratitude the actor's Richard Chevenix, his Rawdon Scudamore, his Jeremy Diddler, his Bill Sikes. He was by no means an ideal Claude Melnotte. Then he fell to playing Doricourt, Charles Surface, Young Marlow, Captain Absolute, drab heroes to a man. But this was only a trial of the die; the gambler's first throw "for love." When it was finally cast, it came down flamboyant. The actor approached his proper goal of the romantic, the fantastic, in Digby Grant, in Jingle, and reached it, amid a roar of astonished applause from the crowd, in Burgomaster Mathias. This was his first great assault on Philistia. It roused the average sensual man to the disquieting consciousness of a nervous system. Contrast it with M. Coquelin's impersonation of the same part, and you have the pass-key to Mr. Irving's method. The one is of imagination all compact, a common Alasatian inn-keeper transfigured by romance, seen, as it were, by flashes of lightning; the other is plausible, logical, correct; a figure of cold daylight, leaving you as cold. In a word, the one is flamboyant; the other only drab.

It was evident from the first that he had not the fluid or ductile temperament which makes your all-round actor, your Betterton, your Garrick. His mind was not like Squire Brooke's, a jelly which ran easily into any mould. Here again his method is antithetic to M. Coquelin's. Universality is the foible of M. Coquelin, who—in defiance of a nose suggesting obvious limitations—thinks with Colley Cibber that "anything naturally written ought to be in every one's way that pretends to be an actor." Mr. Irving's individuality is too strongly marked to let him fall into that heresy. As soon as he attacked Shakespeare we saw that he was not going to sweep the board. He began—of course, they all do—with Hamlet. It is a part in which no actor has ever been known entirely to fail; but it will never be linked with Mr. Irving's name as it is, for all time, with Betterton's— the classic impersonation, "the best part, I believe," says Pepys, "that ever man acted." His Othello, his Richard, were only half-successes. One still prefers to read how Edmund Kean did them. Over the recollection of his Romeo one passes hastily, suppressing a chuckle. His Macbeth, even in its second version, revised and improved, was rather romantic than tragic. So it was in the romantic rather than the tragic repertory of Shakespeare, in the figures painted from the rich fantastic palette of the Italian Renaissance, that one waited for him confidently. Shylock, Iago, Malvolio, Benedick, these are all flamboyant parts, and he took possession of them by right of temperament. To say that his "was the Jew that Shakespeare drew" would be to quote Pope's doggerel inopportunely. It was the Jew idealised in the light of the modern Occidental reaction against the *Judenhetze*, a Jew already conscious of the Spinozas, the

Sidonias, the Disraelis, who were to issue from his loins. His Iago was daringly Italian, a true compatriot of the Borgias, or rather better than Italian, that "devil incarnate, an Englishman Italianate." The remembrance of those grapes which he plucked and slowly ate still sets the teeth of Philistia on edge. His Malvolio had an air of *hidalguia*, something of Çastilian loftiness, for all the fantasy of its cross-gartering; Don Quixote turned Major Domo. Quite the best of his Renaissance flamboyants is his Benedick, as gallant a picture of the courtier-scholar-soldier as anything in the pages of Cellini, or the canvases of Velasquez. But, grateful as we are for these things, his greatest services to Shakespeare, most of us will think, have been less immediate than mediate, less as actor than as manager. Nero did not surpass, nor the late M. Perrin equal, him as a *metteur en-scène*. His series of Shakespearean land and seascapes, Veronese gardens open to the moonlight, a Venice unpolluted by Cook's touristry, groves of cedar and cypress in Messina, Illyrian shores, Scotch hillsides, and grim castles, Bosworth Field—what a panorama he has given us! The sensuous, plastic, pictorial side of Shakespeare had never been seen before he showed it. Here you have the flamboyant artist outdoing Delacroix on his own ground.

Nevertheless, man cannot live by Shakespeare alone, least of all this man. His most permanent triumph has been in melodrama—which is Philistia's name for the stage-flamboyant expressed in prose. His prototype in this was Lemaître; and his conquest of the Lemaîtrist repertory is complete. His Robert Macaire, his Dubosc, are the most effective of stage sudorifics. French melodramas, too, have yielded him Louis XI., the two Dei Franchi, while two of Macready's great parts—played in a manner widely different from Macready's—have furnished him with Richelieu and Werner. These are all studies in the lurid, the volcanic, and they are among his strongest ; but two at least of his best things are figures of repose, if not of still life—his Charles I. and his Dr. Primrose. Over them all, the just and the unjust, his romance has gleamed impartially.

But, as Sainte-Beuve somewhere says, *L'écueil particulier du genre romanesque, c'est le faux*, and this romantic actor could not hope to escape the special danger of his temperament. Like the Don Quixote with whom I have compared him, he has now and then mistaken spavined hacks for Rosinantes and flocks of sheep for armies. His Vanderdecken, his Eugene Aram, perhaps his Philip, and his Count Tristan, were among these errors. His Mephistopheles, too, and, as some think, his Edgar of Ravenswood. The fault was not all his own. His authors played him false. There one touches him between the joints of his harness ; he has failed to create a great modern playwright. Let him crown his career by doing that, and I, for one, will vote for his canonisation. Where is he to find the playwright ? Well, at the risk of passing for a Curious Impertinent, I will hint that a great artist in fiction is to be found under the shadow of a certain hill in Surrey Only to think what the creator of those princely flamboyants, Old Mel and Richmond Roy, might have done—might, surely, still do—for Henry Irving ! As George Tesman says, " fancy that ! "

The Gresham Press,
UNWIN BROTHERS,
CHILWORTH AND LONDON.

TITLES IN THIS SERIES

1   E. F. Benson. *The Babe, B.A.* 1897.
2   A. W. Clarke. *Jasper Tristram.* 1899.
3   Ella D'Arcy. *Modem Instances.* 1898.
4   Frank Danby (Julia Frankau). *Dr. Phillips: A Maida Vale Idyll.* 1887.
5   R. M. Gilchrist. *The Stone Dragon and Other Tragic Romances.* 1894.
6   John Law (Margaret Harkness). *A City Girl.* 1887.
7   Henry Harland. *As It Was Written: A Jewish Musician's Story.* 1885.
8   Averil Beaumont (Mrs. A. W. Hunt). *Thornicroft's Model.* 1873.
9   George Moore. *A Modern Lover.* 1883.
10 W. H. Pollock. *The Picture's Secret.* 1883.
11 William Sharp. *The Children of Tomorrow.* 1899.
12 Count Stanislaus Eric Stenbock. *The Shadow of Death.* 1893.
    bound with *Studies of Death.* 1894.
13 Arthur Symons. *Studies in Seven Arts.* 1906.
14 ———. *London. A Book of Aspects.* 1908.
15 ———. *Amoris Victimia.* 1940.
    bound with *Amoris Victima.* 1897.

16 A. B. Walkley. *Playhouse Impressions*. 1892.

17 Frederick Baron Corvo (Frederick Rolfe). *The Songs of Meleager*. 1937.

18 Evelyn Douglas (John Barlas). *Phantasmagoria*. 1887.
bound with *Love Sonnets*. 1889.

19 Sebastian Evans. *Brother Fabian's Manuscript*. 1865.

20 George Ives. *Book of Chains*. 1897.
bound with *Eros' Throne*. 1900.

21 Eugene Lee-Hamilton. *Gods, Saints and Men*. 1880.
bound with *The New Medusa*. 1882.
bound with *Sonnets of the Wingless Hours*. 1894.

22 Charles Sayle. *Musa Consolatrix*. 1893.

23 Theodore Wratislaw. *Caprices*. 1893.
bound with *Orchids*. 1896.

24 Harry Quilter. *Is Marriage a Failure?* 1888.

25 The Philistine (J. A. Spender). *The New Fiction and Other Papers*. 1895.

LIBRARY OF DAVIDSON COLLEGE

Books on regular loan may be checked out for **two weeks**. Books must be presented at the Circulation Desk in order to be renewed.

A fine is charged after date due.

Special books are subject to special regulations at the discretion of the library staff.